Dandy, Day, and the Devil.

by
James A. Riley

Foreword by Monte Irvin

Original artwork by Jon Houghton

TK Publishers

D1553917

DANDY, DAY AND THE DEVIL

Library of Congress # 87-090021
ISBN 0-96-140232-6

Copyright 1987
TK Publishers
P. O. Box 779
Cocoa, FL 32923-0779
First Printing, February 1987

DEDICATION

To
the players from the Negro Leagues who are deserving
of election to The National Baseball Hall of Fame.

And, especially for
Ray Dandridge, Leon Day and Willie Wells

*. . . I have caused thee to see it with thine eyes, but
thou shalt not go over thither.*

Deuteronomy 34:4

Books by James A. Riley

THE ALL-TIME ALL-STARS OF BLACK BASEBALL

DANDY, DAY AND THE DEVIL

CONTENTS

Monte Irvin as a young professional.

FOREWORD

As the saying goes—There's a time to live and a time to die, but it is also very important to be in the right place at the right time. It's called good timing.

If that had happened to Ray Dandridge, Leon Day, and Willie Wells, how different their lives would have been. Not only would they have established many records in organized baseball but would have achieved fame and fortune for themselves and their families. When hot-stove league fans sit around the fire to discuss the game's greatest performers, their names would be mentioned often and with reverence. In my opinion, they were that good.

But as luck would have it, they were only well known by the followers of the Negro League and in all the Latin American countries that featured baseball.

You see, all three of them were at the top of their game during the middle thirties, and by the time Jackie Robinson broke the color barrier in 1946, Branch Rickey overlooked them because age was against them. Consequently, none of them ever experienced the joy of playing Major League baseball.

Ray Dandridge, better known as "Squatty," was a born third baseman but could play second and short equally as well. He had the quickest reflexes and the surest hands of any infielder I've ever seen. In a season, he had a bad year if he made four errors. As a third baseman, he could field the swinging bunt and get the runner at first better than anyone. It was a thing of beauty and worth the price of admission just to see him make that one particular play.

Most of his career he batted in the number two position because he made real good contact and could hit the ball like a shot to right field on a hit and run situation. Throughout his illustrious career he batted .300 or better.

Next in alphabetical order is Leon Day, the perfect pitcher with blinding speed, great move to first base, and quick as a cat fielding his position. In a must-win situation, the manager always gave the ball to Leon and he failed very few times.

In those important games he would ask his teammates for one run and if they couldn't do it, he would step up to the plate and do it himself. I compare him to Bob Gibson, and if Dwight Gooden continues, he might reach the goals that Leon had accomplished.

Last, but not least, a few words about Willie Wells, "The Devil," as he was called. The opposition would always say, "Don't hit it to shortstop because The Devil is playing out there."

Willie looked like a star ballplayer-had all the actions of an all-star performer-real good hands, quick as could be, and was an expert on catching the short fly ball hit just over his head. He played in close, and in all situations his throw would just beat the runner to first base. It was a science with him.

He could really run and had a lot of power. He averaged 25 to 30 home runs a season and would hit for a high average. You could get him out with a fastball once in a while but he feasted on curveballs. As a fielder, I'd compare him to Phil Rizzuto—as a hitter—Ernie Banks.

The major league fans never had the chance to see these great ballplayers perform, and it's a shame because if they had, they would have never forgotten them.

These fellows were my heroes as I started my career with the Newark Eagles way back in 1937. I don't think I could have picked a better trio because at that time they were the best.

All three of them are still living and should be elected to the Hall of Fame.

My sincere congratulations to the author for giving them the publicity and promotion that they never received but so richly deserve.

Monte Irvin

January 21, 1987

MONTE IRVIN

Monte Irvin was one of the fortunate ones. When the major leagues were opened to black ballplayers, he was young enough to make the transition from the Negro Leagues. Although Monte was 30 years old and his best years were behind him when he broke in with the Giants, he still played eight major league seasons and in two World Series.

Originally, Monte was the choice of the Negro League owners to be the player to break the color line. Had it not been for World War II, he may well have been cast in the role later filled by Jackie Robinson. But fate intervened. While Robinson was playing his only season of black professional baseball with the war-time weakened Kansas City Monarchs, Monte was walking guard duty at a prisoner of war camp in Germany. Consequently, when Rickey made his decision, Robinson was the one chosen for that historic role.

After returning from the War, Monte pioneered the same territory with the New York Giants. Following successful careers in the major leagues and as a Special Assistant to the Baseball Commissioner, it is to Monte's credit that he continues to champion the cause of the players from the Negro Leagues.

INTRODUCTION

Shadows on the Wall

For a half-century, white Americans sat watching major league baseball, only vaguely aware of the shadowy world of black baseball that existed beyond the scope of their vision. To most white baseball observers, black ballplayers were as unreal as the shadows on the wall in Plato's Allegory of the Cave. In this world of reflected images, there existed exceptionally talented players whose ability was unsurpassed anywhere.

Best known to today's baseball world are Hall-of-Famers Satchel Paige and Josh Gibson. But as Satchel himself said, "There were many Satchels, many Joshs." And indeed there were. Required by custom and circumstance to play in their own separate leagues were yesteryear's equivalents of the post-Robinson era's black stars now enshrined in the Hall of Fame.

Today's generations know little about these men who were destined to demonstrate their abilities to a comparatively small segment of American society. During the half-century of dual baseball development approximately 2,650 men displayed their talents in the arenas of black baseball, and many of these were stars whose diamond brilliance shone with such magnitude as to merit selection to the Hall of Fame.

Shadows in the Hall

To date, ten of these deserving stars have been enshrined in the National Baseball Hall of Fame at Cooperstown, New York. In 1971, the Hall of Fame's Special Committee on Negro Leagues selected the legendary Satchel Paige as the first player to receive this honor. A year later, the Homestead Grays' power tandem, Josh Gibson and Buck Leonard, followed their former rival into the brotherhood of the hallowed halls. Over the next ten years Monte Irvin ('73), Cool Papa Bell ('74), Judy Johnson ('75), Oscar Charleston ('76), John Henry Lloyd ('77), Martin Dihigo ('77), and Rube Foster ('81) also were inducted in the Hall of Fame.

When the Special Committee was disbanded, the fate of other deserving players was left to the watch-care of the Veterans Committee and there is legitimate concern that the door has been slammed in their collective faces. With the passing of Satchel in 1982, only four Hall of Fame members remain to represent this generation of players from the black baseball era.

Vanishing Shadows

Annually for a five year period, veterans of the Negro Leagues gathered for a reunion. On those occasions, the mood was festive as players renewed friendships that had previously remained dormant for three decades. But as the fellowship progressed, each year the questions eventually led to the same topic. One player describes this inevitable turn of conversation:

> "We get together and somebody says, 'Where's so-and-so?' And one of us says, 'Oh, he passed.' Then somebody else calls a name and another player says, 'Well, he's passed, too.' Then somebody calls another name and they say, 'He's gone, too.' Then we say, 'It's time to change the subject!'"

This anecdote reflects the very real condition that must be faced. The time will come when there will be no more reunions because there will be no more players to reunite. Each year more names are added to the list of those who have passed away.

The shadows of yesterday are vanishing. And soon there will be no more. The last shadow will disappear, just as did the "days that used to be" that spawned them. A time that is no more and will never be again. But a time that should be remembered—and a time that should be honored.

Three for the Hall

What more appropriate way to honor these men than to grant them their rightful place among the greatest baseball players of their generation by enshrining them in the National Baseball Hall of Fame at Cooperstown, New York.

There is, by conservative estimate, an additional score of players from this era of baseball who deserve this recognition. Most of these are among the shadows who have passed into the history of our National Pastime. But there are three players still with us who unquestionably deserve this honor—Ray Dandridge, Leon Day, and Willie Wells.

When conducting interviews with former Negro League players, certain names were consistently accorded a position of prominence. Everybody had a Satchel story, spoke in awe of Josh Gibson's power, and invariably remembered Buck Leonard as a fine gentleman as well as the greatest black first baseman. Other names that were mentioned with convincing alacrity, were Ray Dandridge, Leon Day, and Willie Wells.

Almost without exception, Dandridge and Wells were named by their contemporaries as the greatest at their respective positions. The older players mentioned them in the same breath as Hall-of-Famers Judy Johnson and John Henry Lloyd, who preceded them by a generation. Leon Day was most often mentioned as Satchel's nearest competitor for honors as the best pitcher of his era. To be rated virtually on a par with Satchel Paige is high praise in its own right. However, in his prime years, Day's performance not only matched, but often surpassed that of the colorful Hall of Fame great.

In addition to being held in high esteem by their fellow players from the Negro Leagues, contemporary press accounts and existing statistics from league play and barnstorming exhibitions offer further evidence of their individual greatness on the ball diamond.

We cannot change the injustices of the past, but we can control the equity of the future. It is time for these magnificently talented players to receive the legacy of their greatness and claim their place in the Hall of Fame. And the accolades should be accorded now, before the last shadow is gone.

Let them smell the roses. . .

DANDY

*"People would pay their way in to the game just to see
him field."*

Monte Irvin

RAY DANDRIDGE

Look at Ray Dandridge today and he looks more like a retired rodeo cowboy than one of the smoothest fielding third basemen to ever play the game of baseball. His bowed legs look like he spent the better part of his life with them wrapped around the sides of a horse, and his muscular torso looks better suited for bulldogging steers than for scooping ground balls out of the dirt. When Ray dons his Stetson he looks like he just stepped out of a Marlboro commercial.

But don't let the looks fool you. This man had hands of velvet and was the greatest third baseman of his generation. Some say that he was the black Brooks Robinson. Others say that Brooks Robinson was the white Ray Dandridge.

Presently, Ray is living the leisurely life of a retiree. When not flipping channels on his large screen TV, he spends his time playing pinochle, watching jai-alai, or just sitting in his front yard and tossing pine cones for his German shepherd, Pepper, to catch. She goes back on the pop-fly pine cones just like her master used to half a century ago. Ray has also taught her to catch short-hops and grounders, as well.

I first met Ray in the summer of 1981 at his home in Newark, New Jersey, that he bought with the big pesos advanced as inducement for him to perform his glove magic under the Mexican sun. Ray popped a few tops while we spent an afternoon talking about a career that spanned twenty-three years and half of the globe. Later we adjourned to his basement where the memorabilia from his career as a baseball nomad was soon spread out over his pool table. The task of assimilating the mountainous montage of baseball history into a workable document was over-

3

whelming. And even then the surface was still only barely scratched. What did emerge, however, was a profile of one of the greatest third basemen in the history of baseball.

Monte Irvin, who played with and against Dandy in four different countries, shakes his head in awe when remembering the diamond exploits of the man with the velvet hands. "Dandridge and Wells were two of the finest infielders I've ever seen," he states without reservation. "I'm talking about bar none. I've seen Rolfe, I've seen Robinson, I've seen Graig Nettles, I've seen all the great third basemen. But I've never seen anybody who could make the plays any better than Dandridge."

"And once you saw him you'd never forget him because he was short and bowlegged. But he was quick as a cat and he had an adequate arm. If the ball got to him real quick, he would always time it so that his throw would just beat you. When he had to hurry it was the same way, the throw would just beat you. He was the best I've ever seen on a swinging bunt. Because he was already short and he'd come in full speed, take that ball and toss it underhand and just get you. It was a thing of beauty just to see him come in and flip that ball underhand without even slowing down on it. It was the damnedest thing I've ever seen."

"You know, it's hard to describe his style of fielding. You had to see him play. People would have paid just to see him play third base. He was something! The way that he went after a ball . . . the way that he would backhand a ball with that big glove of his . . . and the way he would come up with a hard hit ball . . . and he'd take it and shake it before he'd throw it to first base."

"I saw him and I have so much respect for him. He was very spectacular but not showy, understand. Certainly not a showman in the way he fielded like Willie Mays with the basket catch. But something about the way he moved made him separate and apart from all the rest of the third basemen. They loved him in Mexico. They thought he was the best third baseman in the world. They still talk about him." Monte pauses momentarily to reflect, and then concludes with finality, "Dandridge was one of the best ever."

One of the best ever! And yet in his playing days, because of his skin of ebony, the doorway to the major leagues was closed to Ray. Now, the door to the Hall of Fame also seems to be closed to him. For several years he has missed election by a narrow margin. Baseball authorities who have seen him play agree that he should already be enshrined. The standards for the Hall of Fame are self-defining, but if players of Ray's stature from the Negro Leagues continue to be excluded, the integrity of the institution will be seriously compromised.

Ray Wandridge

The August sun warmed the overflowing throng of baseball fans who had jammed into the little New York village of Cooperstown to witness the Baseball Hall of Fame's induction ceremonies. Among the 1984 inductees were two third basemen, Brooks Robinson and George Kell.

Robinson is considered by many baseball authorities as the greatest all-around third baseman ever to play the game. A perennial gold glove winner at his position, he was selected to *The Sporting News'* American League All-Star team nine times between the years 1961-1972. Prior to Robinson's brilliant career, the man generally acknowledged as the greatest all-time third baseman was Pie Traynor. In the pre-expansion era when *The Sporting News'* selections reflected a combined major league All-Star squad, the Pittsburgh great earned that distinction seven of the first nine years that the team was selected (1925-1933). Later George Kell won the same recognition from *The Sporting News* six times over a seven year period (1946-1952).

Between the reigns of Traynor and Kell, the best third baseman in baseball was a stocky, bowlegged magician with a glove, named Ray Dandridge. Ray could field like Brooks Robinson and hit like George Kell. Yet their plaques were being placed in the marbled halls at the National Baseball Hall of Fame while, for the third consecutive year, Ray missed election by a narrow margin. How complete it would have been to have inducted the entire triad of third base greats into the Hall at the same time. But it was not to be on this summer day.

As the ceremonies got under way, Wild Bill Hagie led the disproportionately partisan Baltimore crowd in his famous O.R.I.O.L.E.S. cheer. When Robinson, the Baltimore great, was introduced the crowd went wild. George Kell, who closed out his career with the Orioles, asked for a share of the Baltimore celebration. The festive occasion was well deserved for both of these gentlemen who were the best of their respective generations at the hot-corner.

But absent from the jubilation was the other great third baseman who also was the best of his generation, Ray Dandridge. Consigned by the color of his skin to a career outside the major leagues, his prime years were spent laboring in the relative obscurity relegated to the Negro Leagues and the Mexican League.

Hall of Fame outfielder Monte Irvin, who played with Ray in both of these leagues prior to joining the New York Giants, offers his endorsement of Ray Dandridge for the Hall of Fame. "Ray was one of the greatest ever. He was a legend in Newark. He had the greatest hands I've ever seen. He was fantastic. He was such a great fielder that people would pay their way in to the game just to see him field. He had that style. It's just a crime that people never got to see him play in the major leagues."

◊   ◊   ◊

In the States his teammates called him "Dandy" and "Danny," while opposing players called him "Squatty" and "Hooks." In Cuba the fans called
him "Talua," and in Puerto Rico and Mexico he was called "Mamerto."
But by whatever name he was called, wherever he went, in whatever
league he played, there was none better at the hot-corner than the man
with the velvet hands.

It was said that a train could run between his bowed legs but a
baseball never got through them. At Newark in the Negro National
League, Ray teamed with another bowlegged whiz, shortstop Willie
Wells, to form an almost impregnable left side of the infield. Joined with
the right side combination of Dick Seay at second base and Mule Suttles
at first base, they formed the million dollar infield. This designation was
based on their baseball value had they been white.

After playing the better part of the thirties with Abe Manley's
Newark Eagles, the lure of better pay, more favorable living conditions,
and status as a first-class citizen finally led to Ray leaving Newark and
heading south of the border to Mexico where he spent the larger part of
the next decade.

When Branch Rickey's scouts were bird-dogging the hemisphere in
search of the right man to break the color line in the major leagues, Ray
was considered for that distinction. Dodger manager, Tommy LaSorda,
who played with Ray in Cuba underscores this point. "When they were
talking about bringing Robinson to the major leagues, a lot of people
thought they should have brought up Ray instead. That tells a lot about
how good he was. He's the best third baseman I ever saw in my life."

While Robinson was still a rookie shortstop with the Kansas City
Monarchs, Ray was batting .366 to lead the Mexico City Reds to a pennant. In his capacity as playing manager Ray was earning $10,000 a year
and he could not give up that security in exchange for the uncertainty that
faced anyone in the role as the first in Rickey's noble experiment. During
that championship season Ray also set the Mexican League equivalent of
the Joe DiMaggio record for hitting safely in the most consecutive games,
29. In honor of the occasion, Jorge Pasquel, who doubled as the team
owner and league president, had his manager present Ray with a trophy
bearing the inscription, "He came, he conquered." While Jackie Robinson
was breaking the color barrier in Montreal and Brooklyn, Ray was having
two more all-star seasons with Mexico City where he registered batting
averages of .323 and .329, respectively.

Bill Veeck and other major league moguls were still interested in him
but Ray still didn't want to make the break under the existing conditions.

7

*Ray Dandridge with Tomma LaSorda and Sandy Koufax in Vero Beach,
Florida—1985.*

"Bill Veeck of Cleveland wanted me to come out of Mexico during the
time that Jackie Robinson was trying out for the Dodgers," Ray remembers. "I was down there with that Pasquel gang and Pasquel was paying
me $10,000 a year and I had all my expenses paid and I had my family
with me. Bill Veeck wrote me a letter and wanted me to try out for his
team at that time but he didn't offer me no kind of bonus or nothing. And
I asked them, 'Is there any kind of bonus or anything that I can get?' I
knew that ballplayers were getting bonuses to go on to the major leagues
and they wouldn't give us anything. They didn't want to give us a bonus.
I said, 'I'm not taking that chance.' Because I was making good money in
Mexico. I had worked all the way up from $350 a month to $10,000 a
season. I was making a nice salary and was well taken care of, and Veeck
wouldn't give me a guarantee. I thought I would be jeopardizing a whole
lot, so I refused. I wouldn't jump." Consequently Ray stayed another year
and, in addition to his usual sterling defensive play, led the league with a
.373 batting average.

8

Meanwhile Veeck had signed Larry Doby to an American League contract and, contrary to the policy of other owners who placed their emphasis on youth, also signed Satchel Paige who was reputedly "older than dirt." Encouraged by these trends at home and saddened by the death of his benefactor, Jorge Pasquel, who was killed in a plane crash, Ray returned to the States as player-manager of the New York Cubans.

Early in June while playing in Petersburg, Virginia, Ray received a call from the Cubans' owner Alex Pompez and was informed that he and pitcher Dave Barnhill had been sold to the New York Giants. "He said 'The Giants need a second baseman and a pitcher. How would you like to come back to New York?'" Ray didn't even hesitate. "I told him, 'I'd love it!' And he said to pack my bags and come right back to New York." So Ray appointed Pat Scantlebury as interim manager of the Cubans, and the Giants' new acquisitions caught the first train back to New York. No sooner had the two ballplayers arrived in the metropolis than they had to leave again. The Giants had assigned them to their highest farm team, the Minneapolis Millers in the AAA American Association. Ray just had time to go home to Newark to see his family before he and Barnhill jumped a plane bound for Minneapolis.

Meeting them at the airport was Minneapolis' general manager Rosy Ryan, who took them, suitcases and all, straight to Nicollet Park. By the time they got to the locker room and into their uniforms, it was the bottom half of the eighth inning in the first game of a Sunday doubleheader. Future Red Sox star left-hander Mickey McDermott was pitching for the visiting Louisville ball club and was in the process of striking out 18 batters in the game. Manager Tommy Heath turned to Ray and asked "Do you think you can hit him?" Ray assured him, "Well Skip, that's what I came up here for. I know you didn't call me up here to sit on the bench." Heath said "Well get your bat and try it."

Ray selected his timber and stepped into the batter's box but he didn't stay there long. The first pitch was right at his head and he had to hit the dirt. "I knew what to expect when I got up to the plate," Ray affirms as he tells the story today. "So I went up there and McDermott was on the mound and *I know* . . . *I know* . . . See I've been playing a good while against whites back in Cuba and Mexico. I know good and well a black man coming up to bat the first time in their league . . . I know I'm going to have to eat dirt. I knew what I had to do and I got prepared for it. So . . . it was true . . . my thoughts were right . . . and boom! . . . there I go . . . I went down. The first one that he threw was right at my head to make me get in the dirt . . . so I got in the dirt. Then I got back up and I stood there and I said to myself, 'Well I know he's already got his kicks now. He's done got his thrill. I don't think he'll throw at me again, so I'm going to see what he's got.' And I said, 'Now bring it on in.' So here he comes with another fastball that looked like it was 100 miles an hour."

But Dandridge was ready for it, and drilled a line drive back through the box that McDermott knocked down in self defense. "I made him duck!" asserts Ray. The resilient veteran had made his point. They knew that he was a ballplayer and couldn't be intimidated. "So from then on I started playing in Minnesota," he says. "From then on I didn't look back. I was a player with them."

That is an understatement! Ray did the seemingly impossible and made it appear routine. Rosy Ryan got a quick glimpse of the magic in Ray's oversized mitt in the second game of the doubleheader when Ray, who started at second base, made a sensational play on a slow roller that trickled out between first and second. Ray charged the ball, engulfed it in his massive glove and flicked it to the first baseman to rob the batter of a base hit. Watching from the press box, Ryan exclaimed, "How in hell did he get the ball out of that gladstone bag so fast?"

Before Ryan's credulity was completely restored, the second batter hit a ball up the middle that further showcased the extent of Ray's range afield. "I had to go a long ways to get it," he recalls. "When I wound up I was way behind the pitcher and I threw the batter out." Ray was constantly pulling outs from the bag of tricks that he wore on his left hand. And he also had a knack for timing his throw so that he always nipped the runner by just a half-step. That ability is the one thing that knuckleballer Hoyt Wilhelm, who was Ray's teammate on the Millers in 1950, remembers best about him. "No matter how the ball was hit, he always made the throw so that he just did get the man at first," the Hall-of-Famer reiterates.

"See," Ray explains in agreement, "when you're fielding you've got to know the man that's hitting the ball and you've got to study how fast he can go down that line. Then I'd field the ball and I'd throw it, or lob it, just hard enough to get him. A sports reporter named Holsey Hall was there and he used to say I had a different throw to first base for every play. Like I go behind the pitcher and take a ball, I throw at one speed. If I come in fast on a ball, I throw at another speed and all like that. And always nip the guy by one step."

"I used to say to myself, 'I like to make it an art.' You know, on the throwing part. I could throw the ball hard, I could throw the ball soft, I could throw the ball sidearm or underhand, and if I had to come overhand, I came overhand." The hometown fans were well aware of Ray's variations on his tosses to the initial sack. They had each of them numbered and called out the respective numbers whenever Ray made a play.

"My reputation was, I would come in and just scoop the ball up and throw it, still on the run. Half of the time after throwing the ball, when I'd

Ray Dandridge—The man with hands of velvet.
"No matter how the ball was hit, he always made the throw so that he just did
get the man at first."—Hoyt Wilhelm
(Photo courtesy of Ray Dandridge)

wind up, me and the catcher were so close we could shake hands. And most of the time I got my man at first base."

Ray, a master at fielding bunts, was noted for playing in close when he anticipated the situation. He recalls one time in Cuba when this practice almost proved disastrous. "I knew this guy, he was a good bunter and he was a fast man. So I played in just a little close on him. I was on the edge of the grass and then, when the pitcher got ready to pitch the ball, I walked in on him to try to get the advantage when he bunted the ball. What happened was," Ray explains, "he swung! And he was a left-handed batter and he hit a line drive right at me. And it's a good thing I throwed my hand up in front of my face or it would have tore my jaw all apart. If I hadn't thrown up my hands it would have hit me right in the face. It hit the thumb on my glove hand and knocked it all way back and broke it. When I looked, it was bent all way back behind the back of my hand. So they had to set the whole hand and I was out of the game the rest of the season."

Ray remembers another time when he was playing in on a batter who hit a shot right at him and, once again, the ball was hit so hard that the only thing that saved him was his reflexes. Ray made a diving stop and, while still on his knees, rifled the ball to first. "I knew that if I stood up I couldn't get him," Ray says. "I was on my knees and I threw him out." Naturally, it was by a half-step. "They would ask me how I got rid of the ball so fast and I said, 'That thing's hot. I want to get rid of it, it burns my hand!'"

But the quick release was only part of the picture. Ray was constantly working to find new ways to utilize his God-given skills. He studied each opposing batter and positioned himself accordingly. Ray also scrutinized the different ways that the ball came off the bat so he wouldn't get caught between hops and so he could get a better jump on the ball. "I used to count hops," Ray says. "I would go 'One, two, three, four, . . .', and they would ask me what I was doing. They would say, 'Are you standing out there talking to yourself?' I would say, 'I'm counting every hop that comes to me so I can get it on the right hop."

Ray brought other innovations into the league. "When I went to play in the American Association, I used to use a big glove, almost as big as outfielders use now. But during that time they tried to bar my glove out of the league. They said that I had a mattress," Ray laughs. "I don't know why they wanted to bar my glove out of there. They never complained about my glove anywhere else before that. The only one who complained about my glove was when I was in the American Association with Minneapolis."

The oversized glove and instinctive reflexes afield were trademarks of Ray's game, but the variety and timing of his throwing are what are

most embedded in observers' memories of the hot-corner Houdini. His
control with his throws to first base merely reflected the bat control he
had at the plate. Ray rarely struck out and was such an accomplished hit-
and-run artist that Tommy Heath gave him the green light to give his own
sign for the play whenever he wanted to utilize it as an offensive weapon.

"I used to study the pitcher and I'd say, 'He's going to throw inside
to me. I'm going to hit it.' So if I gave a sign, I'd watch each player and
know which man's going to take the throw because I'm an infielder
myself. You should know who's going to take the throw. I figured if
you're going to put on a hit-and-run play, you've got to hit the ball where
that guy just left. I could hit the ball this side and that side and
everywhere else. That's the reason that I had such a great average. I
didn't hit a whole lot of home runs. Doubles and triples was my main
thing."

Like Yogi Berra, Ray was a notorious bad-ball hitter and he especially thrived on balls thrown up around the bill of his cap. His opponents
learned this the hard way. Later in the year, Louisville pitcher Gordon
Mueller aimed a fastball a foot inside and right at Ray's eyes. Dandridge
simply rocked back on his heels and lined the ball over the right-center
field fence, leaving Mueller on the mound shaking his head in disbelief
and repeating to himself, "No . . . no . . .that's impossible!"

◊　◊　◊

Dandridge and Barnhill were the only two Blacks on the Minneapolis ball
club and as such, they were exploring new territory. Although they were
already friends, the two shared a mutual bond and became closer while at
Minneapolis. "We were good friends and stayed good friends" is the way
that Ray phrases their relationship. For the most part they stayed to themselves, played baseball, and didn't try to force themselves on anyone.

Ray is a very forthright individual and was "telling it like it is" long
before anyone had ever heard of Howard Cosell. And he is still telling it
that way today. "We didn't have any problems with teammates," Ray
says. "When we would go into the clubhouse, if they wanted to sit by
themselves, they could sit by themselves. If you like me, you like me. If
you don't, I don't care. It didn't affect me at all because if I'm going to
play ball, I play anywhere. I don't give a damn. That's the way I've been
playing all my life."

During the time that Ray was at Minneapolis, he often counseled the
young black players who were entering organized baseball. Ray recalls a
time when Larry Doby, who was pioneering the same sociological territory at Cleveland, came to see him about the lack of acceptance that he
was encountering with his Cleveland Indian teammates. "He was down-

hearted," Ray recollects. "He was sitting in my house for at least two or three hours talking. He asked me, 'Ray, how do you make a success with a bunch of ballplayers when, if you do something, they don't even look at you?' I said 'I don't know. You ain't going out there and get the praise in one year. Look, the only thing for you to do is to go out there and play ball. Instead of you concentrating on your baseball, you're trying to concentrate on getting those guys to talk to you. Never mind them talking to you, you try to concentrate on what you're doing.' And Larry went back to Cleveland and that's when he had his greatest year. And he came back that winter and told me 'Ray, you were right. You don't have to go to them, they'll come to you.' And that's what I did when I went to Minneapolis. I did the same thing. I helped break the color line. It was the same in the minors as in the majors. It just didn't get the publicity. But I didn't care."

Ray's philosophy won out over the segregated hotels and restaurants, the knockdown pitches, and the ragging from some opposing coaches. "All that kind of stuff didn't affect me," he reaffirms today. "We knew that in certain towns we couldn't stay with the ball team in the hotels. I think it was Louisville, Kansas City, and one or two other towns that we couldn't stay in the white hotels, and we just had to stay out in the tourist homes. They made all our reservations and we knew that, so it didn't affect us. I don't know how it affected Barnhill but it didn't affect me at all." If it did affect Ray, it was one of the world's best guarded secrets. One press box sage commenting on his relaxed posture on the field observed, "That guy looks like he's waiting for a streetcar."

All Ray did was to stay cool and keep playing the same kind of baseball that he had always played, and people soon began coming to him. He won the affection and respect of fans, opponents and teammates alike with his classy style of play. Before he left Minneapolis he had become the most popular player in town, and the Giants used his local crowd appeal as an excuse to leave him there as a drawing card, rather than bring him up to the majors.

His four years with Minneapolis were the kind from which legends are fashioned. At an age when most ballplayers are comfortably resting in retirement, he finished the first year with a batting average of .362 and copped Rookie of the Year honors. The next season was even more sensational as he was voted the league's Most Valuable Player after hitting .311 with 13 home runs to lead the Millers to the championship.

Using a page out of the Satchel Paige manual, Ray kept them guessing about his age. "When I went up there after I signed with the American Association, they asked me how old I was. I didn't tell them. Didn't nobody know my age," Ray relates. "As long as I was producing, I didn't

want to talk. But every year that I played there, everybody wanted to
know my age. His age was still a mystery when he played in the Min-
neapolis-St. Paul Auld Lang Syne old-timers game in 1967. When asked
how old he was, Ray answered "fifty-three." Rosy Ryan retorted, "Heck,
he was that old when he joined the Millers." Ryan's rejoinder is indicative
of the management's initial skepticism about his real age when he first
joined the organization. When he signed with the Giants he told them that
he was 30 years old. But he was actually 36, and when he won the Silver
Ball, emblematic of the American Association's MVP, he had passed his
38th birthday.

The Millers were in the play-offs that year but after two successive
outstanding seasons, Ray hoped to move up to the parent club since the
Giants were locked in a tight pennant race and also wanted to get into
post-season play. "Now here's the point," Ray emphasizes. "All the
ballplayers knew me. They had played with me and my records show
what I did. And the Giants didn't have a third baseman." But even though
the circumstances logically dictated that Ray deserved a chance at the big
time, once again it was not to be. New York pitching ace Sal Maglie, who
had played against Ray in Mexico, encouraged Giant manager Leo
Durocher to promote Dandridge. "The Barber" informed his skipper,
"You've got the best man in the world in Minnesota, why don't you bring
him up?" But Leo demurred, stating that Ray was "too old to play in the
major leagues." Some baseball men thought that the real reason was that
the major leagues had an unwritten quota system, and the Giants already
had three blacks on their roster, Monte Irvin, Hank Thompson, and Artie
Wilson. Maglie maintains that, with Ray in the line-up, the Giants would
have been the best team in the league. Monte Irvin agrees, "If we had Ray
in 1950, we'd have won the pennant."

The Phillies also wanted the star infielder but the Giants refused to
trade him. For a number of years Ray was bitter about this slight and
made no pretense otherwise, openly responding to questions to that effect.
Even today Ray still feels that they should either have given him a chance
at the majors or traded him to a team that would give him the chance.
"That's the only thing that I *did* resent," he declares. At an old-timers
game in Minnesota during the twentieth anniversary ceremonies celebrat-
ing their 1950 championship season, Giant owner Horace Stoneham kept
Ray up half the night "drinking and talking." During their late-night conversations, Ray expressed those same sentiments to Stoneham. "The only
thing that I don't like about you, Horace," Ray told him, "is that you
wouldn't even give me a chance to go to the major leagues and that was
my goal."

But now he has softened somewhat although he still says, "Not
making it to the major leagues was my biggest disappointment. If I had

made the major leagues, then I would have gone all the way. Even if I didn't stay there no more than one week, then right now I could say that I made it. That I went from scratch, from nothing, to the major leagues. I just wanted to go up there and put my foot in the door so that I could say that I went from the bottom to the top. All the names that people called me didn't bother me as much as the fact I never got my foot in the door."

First it was his color that kept him from getting to the top and then it was his age. But no one ever doubted that he belonged there. When it seemed that they had seen every thing that he could do, Ray would come up with a new bit of magic to impress them all over again.

When the Giants sent Davy Williams down for more seasoning and the heir-apparent to Eddie Stanky couldn't dislodge the ageless wonder from the keystone sack, Tommy Heath was presented with a mild dilemma. He could not bench his most productive player and the front office didn't want their young prospect "riding the pine". Heath asked Dandridge, "Can you play outfield?" Ray responded "No, why did you ask me that, Skip?" When Heath told him about Williams, Ray said, "Well, let him play and I'll sit the bench." But Heath said, "Are you kidding?", and decided to let Williams be the one to sit.

But circumstances alter events, and Heath had an unexpected change in circumstances almost immediately. His third baseman was cut by a sliding baserunner and had to leave the game because of the injury. Heath asked Ray, "Do you think you can play third base?" Ray nonchalantly replied, "Well, I'll go over there and try."

No one knew that was his favorite position. "I guess the guys figured that I had never been there before," Ray reflects. They quickly discovered their error when the first batter dropped a perfect bunt down the third base line and Ray swooped in, fielded the ball and without raising up, threw in one smooth motion to nip the runner at first by a foot. In the dugout Heath jumped up and nearly hit his head on the top of the dugout. "What's he doing now?" the manager inquired increduously. Dave Barnhill, who was sitting beside Heath, just smiled and told him, "You just threw the rabbit in the briar patch." Over thirty years later little Dave still chuckled and his eyes sparkled when he recounted the story. "Nobody was better than Dandridge at third base," he emphasized.

"That was my position," Ray agrees. "I felt like I was right back at my old home. That's when I started playing third base for Minneapolis. Mr. Hubert Humphrey used to come out to see me play." On the Congressman's excursions to the ballpark, he saw plays no one else could make. Once with two runners on base, the batter smashed a ball right across third base that looked like a sure double. But Ray made a diving backhanded stab and, not having enough time to get up and throw the

man out at first, crawled to third base and tagged the bag with his glove
for the force-out. Humphrey enjoyed watching Ray make plays like this
just as much as Ray loved playing in Minneapolis.

"Playing conditions there were different from what I was used to,"
Ray says. "In the Negro Leagues the only way that we could travel was to
travel by bus. A lot of places we would go and play a twilight game and
then we had to go to another town and be there by a certain time for
another game. We didn't have time enough to even take off our uniforms.
We had to undress on the bus and hang our uniform out the window to let
it dry and hope it would be dry by the time we got there. Back during that
time we didn't make but $175 a month. Top notch ballplayers were
making $200-$225 or something like that."

"In the Negro Leagues we used to go out and the lights were as high
as a three-story house. That's where the lights were! If the ball was hit
above the house you had to judge it by yourself and wait until it came
down so that you could see it. I have seen some guys almost get hit in the
side of the head when the ball come down."

"But when we went to organized baseball, it was all different. You'd
take off your uniform and throw it on the floor and come back the next
day and it's clean and you get into it. And when you go from one town to
another, you don't have to worry about nothing. You just get on the train,
go get in the bunk and go to sleep. And the next morning you get up and
you're feeling good. I thought that was the best thing that ever happened
to me."

"Those guys from the white leagues couldn't play in our Negro
Leagues because they couldn't stand the conditions. To play in Minneapolis was just like we were playing on a mat. I used to have to play in
a cornfield, and now those kids have a mat to play on. It's as smooth as a
piece of paper. Those fields that I had played on were full of bumps and
players trying to field ground balls were getting hit in the nose and getting
their nose busted and still hanging in there. That's the way I came up."

◊   ◊   ◊

And his fellow veteran from the Negro Leagues, Dave Barnhill, came up
the same way. The mound success of Ray's little sidekick caused both of
them to become embroiled in a controversy at Minneapolis. In one game
against Al Lopez' team, fourteen baseballs were thrown out of play because of Lopez' continuous complaints that Barnhill was cutting the ball.
"He got so many guys out that they swore that Barnhill was souping the
ball up," Ray recalls of the allegations. "They had dozens of baseballs
publicized about Barnhill's cutting the ball or doing something with the
ball. Whatever he was doing they never could catch him," Ray asserts,

recounting the incident. "And," he adds, "after they couldn't get it on him, they said that I was doing it at third base." Ray emphatically denies this accusation, but whether or not Barnhill did something to the ball Ray doesn't know. "I asked Barnhill one day and he wouldn't tell me." But if the diminutive pitcher did do something to the ball, he really didn't need to. "Barnhill was one of the best pitchers in the Negro Leagues. We used to call him 'Skinny'. During that time he was great," Ray says without compromise. "He had a good fastball. And he set records in Minneapolis. He was a good pitcher."

Dandridge and Barnhill remained the only black players on the team until the next season, 1951, when they were joined by a young phenom named Willie Mays. In one of John Anderson's country songs he sings, "I'm just an old chunk of coal now, Lord, but I'm going to be a diamond some day." And that's what happened to the three chunks of coal on the Minneapolis squad. Under the heat and pressure that sociological conditions placed upon them, they became sparkling diamonds. Young Willie Mays shone the brightest of the trio and quickly became a superstar.

Ray Dandridge, Dave Barnhill and Willie Mays
with the Minnesota Millers in the American Association in 1951.
(Photo courtesy of Dave Barnhill.)

Ray was partly responsible for the Giants signing Willie. One winter in Cuba, while kneeling in the on deck circle, he noticed general manager Rosy Ryan in the stands trying to get his attention. After his turn at bat, Ray trotted past Ryan's box and said, "What are you doing down here, Rosy?" Ryan, on a scouting trip to see Willie, asked, "How about Mays? Do you think he can play at Minneapolis?" While playing with Willie on the Island Ray had immediately recognized the talented youngster's great potential. "Well if you want that man," he emphasized to Ryan, "you better get right back on the plane and go and get him." Knowing that such great talent can't go unclaimed for long, Ryan respected Ray's advice and Mays became a Giant.

During Willie's short tenure with Minneapolis Ray was able to help him cope with problems that he encountered both on and off the field. He and Tommy Heath took Willie out to center field and showed him how to make the proper throw from the outfield. "He had a hell of an arm but we tried to make him bring his ball down a little lower," Ray says. "That's what we taught him." In addition to helping him hit the cut-off man from the outfield, Ray defended the youngster against efforts at intimidation.

Mays delights in telling one story about how Ray helped him. During a game with Louisville, a 6'5" pitcher named Atkins, knocked Willie down on three straight pitches. While Mays lay sprawled in the dirt, he saw Dandridge advancing towards the mound to confront the towering pitcher. Mays watched apprehensively, thinking "Lord, don't let him hit Ray."

Back in the dugout after the confrontation, Willie asked his protector what he had said to the big pitcher. The described discourse was typical of the Dandridge persona. "I've got two dogs," Ray told the pitcher. "One will go right for your spot when I say 'Bite!'. The other one will sit back and wait until the first one is through and then I'll say 'Bite!' again." In response, Atkins said to Dandridge, "I like you, Ray, but," referring to Mays, "I don't like that little black S.O.B." Ray said, "If you call him that again, I'll sic my *third* dog on you."

In retrospect, Ray doesn't specifically remember this incident, but does concede that it might have happened because that is the kind of exchanges that he sometimes had with people. "A lot of times I said something and I forgot it at that time. Players said that I was crazy, and I guess I was."

Others would say that he was crazy like a fox. Ray was hitting the ball so good at Minneapolis at that time that Heath also asked him to help the younger ballplayers with their batting. Ray told him "If a man wants my help, I'll give it to him. If he don't want it then I'm not going to give it to him."

With Willie, there was not much that Ray or anybody else had to do. God had given Willie Mays all that he needed to be a great hitter. He terrorized the league's pitchers and, unintentionally, put Ray in an uncompromising position. Batting in front of Dandridge, Willie would hit a home run and then Ray would hit a home run. After awhile the league pitchers began to retaliate. Willie would hit a home run and Ray would hit the dirt. Ray went to Heath and said "Skip, if you don't get that man from out in front of me, you're going to get me killed."

Heath didn't have to make a move because the Giants were watching Mays closely and brought him up to the majors after only a month at Minneapolis. When the news came Ray and Willie were together at a theatre. "Me and Willie Mays was sitting in Sioux City, Iowa in a moving picture show", Ray remembers. "And they came on the screen with the message 'Willie Mays wanted at the box office.' I said 'Mays, they want you up at the box office.' He said, 'Man, that ain't for me.' He didn't know it because he didn't see it. So the usher came down the aisle and he said 'Willie Mays . . . Willie Mays.' I said 'I told you that man wants you.' And then he went out to see what it was. So anyhow he came back and said 'Ray, I've got to go to the hotel.' I said 'Well, I'm going to stay here and finish seeing the rest of the picture. I'll see you at the hotel.' And so he went on to the hotel. And when I got back to the hotel, we went to the ballpark and I went on in the clubhouse. Mays would generally be sitting beside me. I said, 'Hey Skip, where's Willie? Where's Mays?' He said, 'Mays is half-way to New York. The Giants called him up!' He said, 'Now you've got to go back to Minneapolis and get his clothes and send them to him.'"

While Willie went on to stardom in the major leagues, Ray was destined to stay at Minneapolis where he finished the year with a .324 batting average and the following season, his last with the Millers, he hit for an average of .294 with 10 home runs. Ray was still the toast of Minneapolis but again he fell victim to circumstances.

"Back then they had a rule that there was only so many years that you could play in the minors and then they had to let you go," Ray relates. "They sold my contract to Sacramento, California in the Pacific Coast League. So I went to Sacramento and then Sacramento made a trade with Oakland and I went to Oakland." While at Oakland, unbeknownst to Ray, a young teenager watched him play and was so impressed that 33 years later, when the two met in Vero Beach, Florida, he would still remember the magic in Ray's glove. The youngster had made a name for himself in baseball in the intervening years. Ray didn't remember Frank Robinson from the Oakland days, but Frank Robinson remembered him. That's when the Hall-of-Famer told Ray how he had watched him as a youngster.

It was during this time at Oakland that Ray's professional baseball career was ended. "That's when me and the catcher collided chasing a foul ball and I hurt my shoulder," Ray relates, remembering the impact on that fateful day. "And I had to sit on the bench because my arm was sore. That was my last year in organized ball."

"I was out of organized baseball the next year. But my arm got better and they wanted me to come to North Dakota. So I went out there and played and hit about .369. I also managed the team and we won it by about 15 games. I stayed there two years, 1954 and 1955. We had a very good ball club out there and then the next year they wanted me to come back but I said, 'Well, being as I can't make it in the major leagues I just may as well give it up.' That's the reason that I gave it up. That's why I quit playing ball."

To hang up the spikes without first being able to stick his foot through the door that Jackie Robinson had left ajar was a difficult decision for Ray. His career had begun at a time when a black man's chances of playing in the major leagues were no more than a prayer and a hope and the dark knight's quest to go "from the bottom to the top" had been a long one.

◊   ◊   ◊

Ray was born in Richmond, Virginia on August 31, 1913. As a youngster growing up, he loved baseball and playing the game came to him naturally. "We used to cut down all the weeds to make a field," he recalls, "and take a branch off a tree and trim it down for a bat, and take a ball and tie a string around it and tape it up to play." When there was no one else to join him in the improvised games, he would practice hour upon hour every day by throwing a ball against a wall, catching it on the rebound and throwing it again. The athletically inclined youngster attended George Mason School in Richmond until the age of ten when he and his sisters moved to Buffalo, New York to stay with their mother.

There he attended an integrated school and was active in sports. Always rough and tumble, he played football, basketball, baseball, and was an amateur boxer. His basketball career was cut short because the coach said that he was "too rough" and dropped him from the team. Ray fared better in the contact sports but after coming home from the boxing matches with a banged up face, his mother encouraged him to discontinue the pursuit of pugilism.

In football, as a halfback, he was always in the middle of the action and took a lot of hard knocks. That was before the days of face masks and other modern protective equipment and consequently, Ray paid the price for being so aggressive. "Every time I came home I would look like

21

a bloody hog," he laughs. In later years Ray continued his football endeavors at a Civilian Conservation Corps camp located a few miles outside Richmond. But after sustaining a knee injury his father advised him to give up the game before he "got all messed up." However, Ray survived the gridiron wars, although the injury required him to wear a knee brace in later years with the Eagles.

In Buffalo Ray continued to attend the city's public school system, including PS#28, until the ninth grade. After dropping out, he still attended vocational school part-time. It was during this time at Buffalo that he first started playing baseball. Initially young Ray played on school softball teams and when he moved to a different section of town in south Buffalo, he naturally wanted to play on the team there. The aspiring youth would go out and just watch the other youngsters play. One day when a player didn't show up, Ray was asked if he wanted to take his place. His response was quick and emphatic, and he proceeded to play shortstop with an enthusiasm that earned him a regular position on the team. Before long, the teenager became the star attraction on the Jacobson and Pharmacy softball team.

His success on the softball diamond eventually led to an offer to play hardball. Of course, Ray jumped at the opportunity. "Yeah, I'll try anything," he answered when asked to try out. He was so excited in his first game that he threw the first ball hit to him completely over the stands. But his desire to play the game quickly overcame his nervousness and for the next two years nothing could keep him away from the baseball diamonds.

After learning the game during his formative years in Buffalo, the eighteen-year-old athlete moved back to Richmond and began playing semi-pro baseball in the sandlots around the area. Each part of town had their own team and he played on the All-Stars, the Violets, and the Paramounts in the Church Hill section. Most towns in the surrounding area also organized ball clubs and city rivalries developed. While traveling with the Richmond team to play in these games, Ray never suspected that two of the players against whom he competed would one day be playing against him in the Negro big leagues. The pair from the Wilson, North Carolina team were Buck Leonard, who is now in the Hall of Fame, and Dave Barnhill, who was destined to later join Ray in breaking the color barrier in the American Association.

Ray looks back on those carefree days of his youth, and tells how it was in semi-pro black baseball and how he first met the two future stars. "I've known Barnhill since before we left home. What I mean by home is, I was in Richmond, Virginia and he was in Wilson, North Carolina. Now we used to play ball against each other before we came up to the

Negro Leagues. He was around there playing and we used to go to Wilson, North Carolina and down in Norfolk and play against him and that's the first time I seen Barnhill."

"Buck Leonard is from down there, too, and he was on the team with Barnhill. They used to play together and we used to play against them. All of us Virginia boys used to go from one town to the other and they did the same. Buck was a great hitter and there was none better at first base. You can't take that away from him."

The sandlots of the eastern seaboard could not long hide Ray's natural talent. One spring day in 1933 the Detroit Stars of the Negro National League came through town while on their way north and, as was the custom of Negro professional teams, played an exhibition game against the local squad. When the Paramounts' shortstop didn't show up, as captain of the team, Ray said "Come on let's play," and proceeded to play shortstop himself. As fate would have it, he had "a beautiful day . . . the best day I ever had in my life." Ray is not bent to exaggeration when he makes this claim. In addition to his play in the field at his new position, the nineteen-year-old ex-center fielder hit a home run off the big league black squad.

Detroit's veteran manager, Candy Jim Taylor, was a superior judge of baseball talent. He was so impressed with what he saw from the promising youngster that he asked him to join the Stars. "The Detroit Stars didn't want to go away without me," Ray affirms. But the local star was not inclined to go. "I didn't want to go nowhere because I had never went away in my life. I didn't even know where Detroit was. I said 'Man, where *is* Detroit?'" But Jim Taylor was not one to take "no" for an answer. That night he found out where Ray lived and brought the team bus by the Dandridges' house to meet his father.

Ray's father, Archie, was invalided by an accident in the textile mill where he had worked. Ray was generally expected to follow his father's footsteps and work in the mill, too. But Archie loved baseball, having been a catcher in his playing days, and he had other ideas.

"Now that's the best part of it," Ray insists, while warming to the topic. Although over fifty years have passed, Ray still recalls that day. "They came to my house. They were asking my father about trying to get me to go away with them. And I hadn't got home. And so later in the day when I did come home my father was telling me, 'Why don't you go ahead on and try it?' I said, 'I don't know where I'm going. I'm going away to Detroit, Michigan and I don't know *where* I'm going.' He said, 'Well the only way you can do it is to try it.'"

"And then I went back out in the street and went to the pool room. I came back from the pool room going home and just about the time I walked around the corner there was a bus sitting in front of the house. I said, 'I ain't going with them. I ain't going.' So I went on back to the pool room and didn't come back until late that night. And I peeped around the corner and there wasn't no bus, so I went on in the house."

When Ray got inside, the elder Dandridge continued to encourage his son to go with Jim Taylor to Detroit. Ray was still unconvinced and asked his father, "Do you really think I can make it?" His father replied, "Why don't you go and try it? You should go on and try it."

The youngster was somewhat reassured but still reluctant to leave home. He asked his father what would happen if he did go with them. "Well," Archie replied, "they're going to pick you up and if anything happens they're going to send you back home." "And" his father added, "they want to give you $60 a month." Ray was still undecided but thinking that the Stars had already gone on to Detroit, he went to bed relieved.

The persistent Taylor had kept his team in town overnight and the next morning, before Ray even had a chance to get out of bed, they were right back knocking at the front door. "My father said, 'Go ahead and pack up a few things, some of your stuff, and go along,'" Ray remembers. "I got a little old straw bag and throwed my stuff in it and I said, 'O.K., I'm going.'" So Ray took his bag and left on the bus with the Stars. He remembers that he had to make good with the team because "when I went to Detroit I didn't have enough to come back."

It wasn't until later that he found out that Jim Taylor had given his father $25 to persuade Ray to go with the team. Or as he says today, "They had done bribed my father and gave him $25 to tell me to go with them. And that's how I managed to start playing ball. That's when I first started my career. But right now, up to this date, I'm kind of glad my father did encourage me to go. I appreciate my daddy telling me to go out and take a chance in the world."

The money that Ray was promised for his first excursion into professional baseball was a far cry from what players today command. Almost all the players of that era played without a formal contract and Ray was no exception. He left home with only a verbal agreement with Jim Taylor. He received the grand sum of $60 a month to play plus an additional $2 a day for "eating money". Such a paltry amount for a quality prospect may leave some of the modern generation a bit skeptical. In agreement, Ray notes, "Now a whole lot of people wouldn't believe that I just made $15 a week when I first went to play baseball."

Now things have changed radically and any player today with any appreciable ability is making a million dollars a year. The spring following Fernando Valenzuela's signing a contract for 1.3 million dollars a year,

Hall-of-Famer Ernie Banks, better known as "Mr. Cub" to the baseball world, proclaimed to all who would stand still long enough to listen "One point three million is not anything today. A million dollars ain't nothing!" Ray agrees that the salaries have gotten out of hand. "There's one ballplayer who makes more in one season than I made in twenty-some years. That's ridiculous! I've been half-way around the world and I ain't made a million dollars yet." But the finances of black baseball in those bygone years were shaky at it's best, and in the depths of the depression money was even harder to come by.

Many players fell victim to the economics of the times and quit baseball for the security of a regular job. During Ray's first season he had to make that decision about his baseball career. In contrast to the uncertainty of making a living playing baseball, he was offered a steady job that paid twelve months a year.

"There's a big story there," he says recalling the opportunity. "I was in some sawmill place down there in Laurel, Mississippi and I don't know how many miles I was from home. And the guy wanted to give me a job and give me a salary for the whole year around to stay there and work in a paper mill. He was going to pay all my expenses and pay my lodging, and I was going to accept it. But I went back to where we were staying in a rooming house and I said, 'Where *am* I anyway? I don't even know where I am and this guy here says he's going to give me a job way down there in the woods by a paper mill place.' I thought about that and I looked in the paper and I was 900 miles from home. I said, 'What am I thinking about?' And I canceled that baby!" That was Ray's first crucial career decision and he is glad that he resisted the temptation to take the guaranteed income.

Ray had good reason to have given serious consideration to the proposition because the Stars' financial situation soon deteriorated to the point where they were unable to pay even the $15 a week that they had promised. At the end of the season the Detroit team dropped out of the league, disbanded, and had to pawn their team bus to get enough money to send the players home. Ray took a bus back to Richmond and the next year, when they called and wanted him to come back again, he steadfastly refused to rejoin the team.

But Ray never regretted leaving home to play that first professional season in Detroit. The reason was the man with whom he left, Candy Jim Taylor. He credits Taylor, who deserves his reputation as a good teacher of baseball, with being the one who made him into a good hitter. Ray likes to relate the story of how the veteran manager performed this transformation. "I started out in 1933 with the Detroit Stars as an outfielder when I was 19 years old. When I was coming up and playing in my hometown, I used to try to be a home run hitter. I thought I was a home run king. Then when I went to Detroit and started playing with those fellows who really knew how to play, they cut that home run down, you know. So Jim Taylor taught me how to hit line drives."

"We were traveling around in that bus and when we got to Laurel, Mississippi we went out to the ballpark to practice. The manager, Candy Jim Taylor, said, 'Kid, you're swinging too hard and you're not timing the ball. Don't try to be a home run hitter or you'll strike out a lot because you have to swing a little harder. Come here, I'm going to show you how to hit. Now watch me. I want you to practice this.'"

"I stood right behind the batting cage and watched. He stepped up to the plate and had the pitcher throwing the ball. He said, 'Now look, the pitcher's going to throw the ball inside.' And he hit the ball to the left side. Then he said, "Now watch, he's going to throw one straight down the middle. I'm going to hit it to center field.' And the pitcher threw one down the pike and he hit it right over the pitcher's head to center field. Then he said 'Watch it, he's going to throw one outside. I'm going to hit it to right field.' And he did!"

"He was naming the spots where he was going to put it at. I said, 'Now how can he do that? If it was me I'd be trying to pull the ball. I don't see how in the world he can hit that ball like that.' So he said, 'Now you come up and try it'. I'm a youngster. I'm a rookie and I say to myself, 'Listen, I can do it too.' And in my mind I say, 'If he can do it, I think I can do it too.'"

"I used to use a light bat, about 33 ounces in weight. He said, 'You don't use this kind of bat.' And he took my bat and threw it away on the side and gave me a bat that seemed to me like it weighed a ton compared to the one that I had been using. That bat that he gave me to use was a big sucker, a 37 ounce bat. And he kept me out there for a solid week with that heavy bat."

"He said, 'Now don't keep wiggling your bat, just take your time and watch that pitcher throw the ball. Keep your eye on the ball.' And then I started getting the swing of it, and that's when I could hit the ball any place I wanted. I got so that after I played several years more, I could hit a pitch anywhere I wanted, and that's how I managed in my career to become so good in hitting."

"If the ball was inside, hit to left field. If the ball was right down the heart of the plate, hit the ball back through the middle to center field. If the ball is outside, step into it and hit the ball to right field. And it just stuck in my mind. I did that and right today I don't mind telling nobody that that man made me a hitter. Candy Jim Taylor! I can't ever forget that man."

"And every year you can see my records and I hit over .300. If you're hitting .300, you're hitting pretty good. The most home runs I ever hit in my life from then on was 13, and that was the year at Minneapolis when I was the Most Valuable Ballplayer in the league."

◊   ◊   ◊

Candy Jim Taylor was not the only baseball personality whose experience and knowledge of the game benefited the rookie. Ray was eager to improve himself and determined to learn everything that he possibly could about the game of baseball. Having always played "out East" before joining Detroit, he didn't know anyone when he first came up in the western league. But the amicable youngster readily became acquainted and learned from other veteran players. "When I was a rookie we would sit outside the hotels at night," Ray says, recalling those early days. "And I used to sit and look at other ballplayers and I'd hear the old-timers talk about each ballplayer around the league. You know, talk about what this ballplayer could do and what that ballplayer could do. And they were telling me one time that ballplayers could catch a ball going this way and catch a ball and throw it back that way and such. I'm sitting there, a rookie, and I ain't saying nothing. But I say to myself, 'I don't believe that.' So the next day I used to go out when we had practice and I'd say 'I'm going to see if that can happen.' And it could happen. That's where I learned a lot about fielding and everything else."

"And I had a couple of guys who helped me," Ray adds, telling how he gleaned useful information from the experiences of others. "I used to wait for the ball to take another hop, and a lot of those guys would beat it out. Jud Wilson, who played at Philadelphia when I was a rookie, used to tell me, 'When the ball makes a big hop, always come in on it.' I tried and it came out good and I was getting those guys out. Now this guy on another team is telling me how to field and I'm listening and learning. I used to listen unless I found out that what they said was wrong. Because a couple of balls made a big hop and I would come in and get the ball and then I can throw him out. So I started charging that ball, coming in and taking it on the short hop and things like that. And I started throwing like that and I got everybody out. And that's the reason I don't doubt anything. If anybody wants to teach me anything, I'm going to try it out and see if it works. I ain't doubting anybody's word. Not those old-timers. Because some of those old-timers were *great*. Believe me, if I tell you!"

After that first season with Detroit Ray returned to Richmond, but not for long. Dick Lundy, one of the all-time greatest shortstops in baseball history, was the playing manager of the Newark Dodgers. His prime years were behind him and he needed someone to spell him at shortstop. "So he came to Richmond, Virginia and asked me if I wanted to go down and take a chance with him", Ray relates. "To stop in Virginia and pick me up like that, somebody had to have recommended me. Bob Evans and I lived about two blocks apart and I said, 'Are you going to take me and Evans together?' Lundy agreed to take him too, so we went down to spring training with him. When we arrived the third baseman hadn't showed up so he told me, 'You practice at third and I'll play short until this fellow gets back.' And I played it so good that later when the third baseman showed up, Lundy told him, 'You don't have a job. You can go on back home, I've already got a third baseman.' Now, that's how I started playing third base."

Newark's new third baseman hit a cool .333 for the second division Dodgers, and began to earn a reputation for himself as the best third baseman in the league. The following year, although the Dodgers dropped to the league's cellar with an abysmal winning percentage of .293, the twenty-one year old budding star earned a spot in the second annual East-West game, the Negro Leagues' all-star extravaganza.

◊   ◊   ◊

During this time when Ray was breaking in with Newark, the Pittsburgh Crawfords were the dominant team in black baseball and fielded a team consisting of five future Hall-of-Famers. Most baseball historians consider them to be the greatest team in the history of the Negro Leagues. They boasted a lineup that included the best pitcher, greatest slugger, and fastest baserunner in the sport. Those luminaries being, in respective order, Satchel Paige, Josh Gibson and Cool Papa Bell. Ray liked playing against the great Crawfords. "I've played against most every ballplayer there is that's got a name," he likes to remind everyone. Although Ray respected the special talents of this great trio, the player that he liked to watch most was their smooth-fielding third baseman, Judy Johnson. Until Ray came on the scene Judy was generally regarded as the best in the league at the hot corner. This quartet of superstars were managed by the great Oscar Charleston who, in deference to his age and added weight, had moved to first base but was still a devastating hitter.

But Newark's cocky young third baseman was not in awe of these legendary greats. Once at Pittsburgh in between games of a doubleheader against the Crawfords, when Satchel Paige was scheduled to start the second game, Ray and Willie Wells challenged the great moundsman, telling him what they were going to do to him in the second game. Ray calls this practice "woofin'."

Dandy (center) and The Devil (left) woofin' at the opposition in Mexico.
Josh Gibson (right) and fans seem to be enjoying the proceedings.
(Photo courtesy of Ray Dandridge.)

"We had gone out there and beat them the first ball game and in the locker room they just had a partition between the two sides and we had to stand on some boxes so we could look right over the top. Me and Wells were jiving, you know, looking over the wall and hollerin' at Satchel 'Come on out there, you're next! You say you throw so hard, we'll see.' Satchel didn't answer back. He just sat there laughing and looking at us, and went on putting on his shoes and getting dressed. It was just one of those things. Me and Wells ribbed a whole lot of teams that way in the clubhouse. That's the way we used to do it. We were just joking, you know."

But when the teams took the field it was no joke. "We went out there and Satchel was throwing the ball like it was a pea," exclaims Ray. The first time that he came to bat, Satchel aimed one of his famous fastballs right under his antagonist's chin, sending Ray into the dirt. Undaunted, Ray got up, brushed himself off, and rapped the next pitch for a base hit. "You had to have guts to play," Ray explains. But adds quickly, "Satchel didn't throw at you. Maybe he'd throw a close pitch to get you back from the plate, but I played with him on all-star teams and played against him and I've never seen Satchel throw at a man." With the velocity that he had he didn't have to resort to knockdowns. "He was getting everybody out," Ray continues. "And it started raining and everybody was glad," he laughs, "because Satchel was bearing down."

The only other contemporary pitcher who could compare with Satchel was the St. Louis Cardinals' fabulous Dizzy Dean. After the 1935 season, Ray joined Satchel and Josh Gibson to barnstorm against Dizzy and his brother Paul. "Back during that time the *Daily News* was comparing ball clubs together and barnstorming and everything else," Ray explains. "So we picked an all-star team and Dizzy Dean picked an all-star team and we started barnstorming with each other. We used to play exhibition games in the Polo Grounds and Yankee Stadium at the end of the season. That's how we managed."

The brother combination had accounted for 49 wins between them in pitching the Cardinals to a pennant the previous year, but Ray was not awed by them any more than he had been by Satchel. "I hit against Dizzy, and Dizzy used to throw hard," he says, "but I got the bat on the ball. I've never been intimidated by anybody. I didn't care who he was," he insists. "I hit all of 'em." The record confirms Ray's confidence. In one game of the October series Ray registered three hits in four plate appearances."

Dizzy was in his prime and was the major crowd attraction, but the competition was evenly matched. "We had an all-star team too, so we used to play some pretty good games," Ray declares. "Back during that time we had Satchel Paige on our team, and Johnny Taylor. "And they used to have some close ball games, 2-1 and like that. Sometimes Satchel used to beat Dizzy this week, one-to-nothing and Dizzy would come back and beat Satchel the next week one-to-nothing. I don't know who threw hardest. It would be hard to say, but I think Satchel threw harder than Dizzy back during that time before he hurt his arm."

"You know he hurt his arm down in Santo Domingo. Before that Satchel really didn't need no curveball. Because I played on a team with Satchel and he called the outfielders in and had his infielders sit down and walked three men intentionally and then he'd strike out three batters. And right now, a whole lot of people don't believe this."

Satchel's opposing number on the barnstorming tour would have readily believed it. Ol' Diz later was quoted as saying "I know who's the best pitcher I ever did see, and it's old Satchel Paige, that big lanky colored boy." The Cardinal great also told Satchel that if he had been on the Cardinals with the Dean brothers, they would have "won the pennant by the fourth of July and gone fishing." Ray concurs with that assessment and laughs "maybe they could have gone fishing even sooner."

The barnstorming was a prelude to the time when Ray began playing ball the year around. After the 1935 season he went to Puerto Rico with an all-star team that played under the banner of the Brooklyn Eagles and included Buck Leonard, Vic Harris, Leon Day, and Raymond Brown.

Two years later, Dolph Luque took him down to Cuba where the flashy fielder promptly proved himself with a .299 batting average, while leading the league in stolen bases. The Cuban ballparks were great for playing, and the people there knew the game and appreciated the finer points of play. The weather and social conditions were beautiful and Ray liked the tropical island so much that he spent a total of eleven winters in Luque's native land. Luque, a former pitching star for the Cincinnati Reds, was a tough hombre. Ray recalls that the Latin ace kept a gun in a desk drawer in his office, and frequently carried it in his hip pocket to enforce team discipline.

One winter, a rival league formed and even the pistol couldn't keep players from switching teams. "That year, I think it was 1947-48," Ray recalls, dipping into his bag of memories, "we jumped from Luque's club to go to a club in another league. They were making up a new league and they wanted some of the ballplayers to come over there to play. So we all got together and went over to this league. I think it was about ten ballplayers."

Luque and the owners of the teams in the established league didn't look with favor on the jumpers. "During that time I thought everything was going along smooth and things were alright. Then they started taking the ballplayers who jumped from one club to another to the jail. They ganged them all up and took them down to the police headquarters. The entire team was arrested. It happened that I was out that day, and when I come back I asked, 'Where are all the guys?' And he said 'Well, they done got all of them and took them down to the police headquarters.' So, then I took a trip to the jail. I got a taxi and went down there, and I went to the police headquarters and I said, 'You all looking for me?' And they said, 'Yeah, Talua, where you been? We been looking all over Havana for you.'"

"After they got out, the new league only lasted about six weeks and when it broke up, the team folded and all the ballplayers who went over to that league were barred from the regular league in Cuba. And then I went from Cuba to Sonora, Mexico and I played there for a season. So during that time the teams got together and reached an agreement. And I got a telegram from Cuba, that they were going to reinstate me. That's when I went back to Cuba. I was reinstated the following year."

Cuba was not the only exotic land that beguiled the footloose infielder. Ray became so well acquainted with the western hemisphere that he could have opened a travel agency. Ray checks off the names of the places where he has played, "I went there to Cuba and then I went to Sonora, Mexico and went down to South America. I went to Puerto Rico quite a few years. I been all through the Caribbean Sea, Santo Domingo, and to almost all those places that played baseball at that time."

After the 1938 season with Newark, Ray was offered $350 a month to go to Venezuela to play for Caracas. Since he was only making $150 a month at the time, he agreed to go if they would give him a two-month advance. When he went to the bank to pick up the money, he stuffed it in both of his front pockets and kept both hands stuck in his pockets to keep from losing it on the subway ride home. He was so concerned with not losing the money that he missed his exchange and had to ride all the way back and start over again. When he finally got home he spread the money out all over the bed. "It was more money than I had ever seen in my life," Ray declares. He didn't even know where Venezuela was, but he showed his wife the money and said, "I'm going to play ball there." Ray took $100 for himself, left the rest for his wife, and boarded a boat for South America.

At that time, Ray didn't know anyone on the southern continent but on the boat he met a black couple and, after getting acquainted, found that it was the Pittsburgh Crawford's former star left-hander, Leroy Matlock, and his wife. He and Matlock became friends on the trip down, and after they arrived they found another American refuge from the Negro Leagues, Harry Williams. The three Americans were the best players on the team and became good friends while playing in Venezuela. The playing fields there were bad and the equipment was bad, but the money was good and "it was a living."

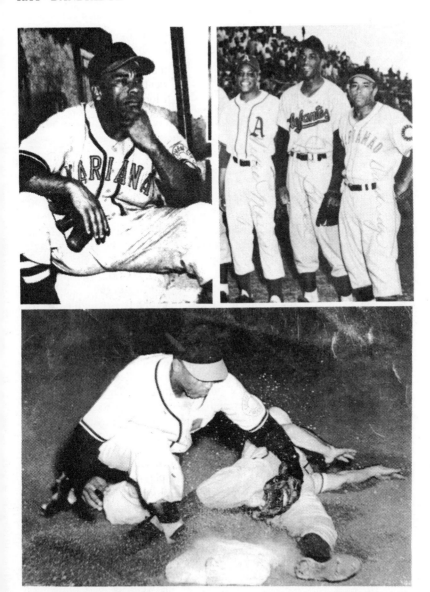

*Ray played 11 winters in Cuba. The Island favorite strikes a pensive pose
in the dugout (top left), poses with Willie Mays and Joe Black
(top right), and puts the tag on a baserunner (bottom).*
(Photos courtesy of Ray Dandridge.)

Ray stayed in Caracas for two years and during his stint in South America, he experienced one of his most memorable seasons. In 1939, he went to Venezuela in August and led Caracas to a title. Afterwards, with six weeks still left in the season, he traveled to Mexico and led Vera Cruz to a title there. Then in October he stopped off in Cuba and almost pulled off another miracle with Cienfuegas, but fell just a half game short of a title there. The narrow miss at his third flag in twelve months was no fault of Ray's, as he topped the .300 mark for the second consecutive season, slapping out a .310 average on the heels of .319 the previous year.

◊   ◊   ◊

This was during the halcyon years with the Newark Eagles that had begun in 1936 when Abe Manley bought the franchises of two losing teams, the Newark Dodgers and the Brooklyn Eagles, and consolidated them into one ball club with a new name. The birth of the Newark Eagles launched a decade of quality baseball for the Manley organization. "That's when they started getting more popular," Ray acknowledges.

Like most of the owners in the Negro National League, Abe Manley made his money in the numbers racket. Ray didn't care what he was doing "as long as he was giving me my money. Back during that time I kept out of everybody's business. The Manleys treated me nice."

Manley was a gregarious man who "loved baseball". He liked to spend time around the club where the ballplayers "hung out" when they weren't playing baseball and, pitcher Leon Day recalled, he played poker with them "like a quarter was a hundred dollars." The Eagles' owner liked just being with the players and even traveled on the bus with the team. "He used to go to all the ball games with us," Ray recalls. "One night we was coming from Harrisburg and the bus went out of control and we went through a gas tank and hit a house and was going down a hill and went through a man's store and the bus was hanging down in the cellar. But nobody got hurt. Mr. Manley was in the bus, too. And we got out of the bus, and stayed there all night. The next morning when we got up it was daylight, and come to find out we were hanging over a cliff!"

"He died early, you know," Ray adds about the Eagles' owner. "When he died I was in Mexico." After Manley's death, his wife Effa took control of the team. The transition was smooth, however, since even before his demise, Effa had handled the team's business matters. Although Mrs. Manley was a practical business woman and was instrumental in developing a team that annually challenged for the title, her involvement in management sometimes caused friction between herself and members of the team. She was noted for telling the managers who to play on certain occasions. One of her personal favorites was pitcher Terris

In Venezuela, Ray displays his batting technique (left).
The gifted gloveman starred with Caracas in 1939 (top right) and 1940 (bottom).
(Photos courtesy of Ray Dandridge.)

McDuffie, and she liked to show him off for members of her ladies' club. "She was very active," Ray states. "Every game we played she came in the dugout. She liked to be around the players." However her penchant never kept the Manleys from fielding a good ball club.

When Gus Greenlee divested himself of the Pittsburgh Crawfords in 1936 to pay off a hit in his numbers racket, Cum Posey's Homestead Grays moved to the forefront as the premier team in the Negro National League. But their perch at the apex of the league was not uncontested and a heated rivalry emerged between the Grays' and Manley's Eagles for league dominance. Year in and year out the Grays and Eagles battled tooth and nail. "We liked to beat the Grays," Ray says, "because they had the name. They thought they were the king of the mountains."

Knockdown battles, slashing baserunning, brawls, and near riots were not uncommon occurrences when the two teams squared off. The Grays had the power tandem of Josh Gibson and Buck Leonard, who were called the Babe Ruth and Lou Gehrig of black baseball. But the Eagles had the million dollar infield to counter them.

"During that time when I played with the Newark Eagles, the Homestead Grays and the Pittsburgh Crawfords were supposed to have been the best black teams, but we thought we were the best," Ray remembers. "Because we had a million dollar infield. That was in 1937 that we had the infield together. I was playing third base, Willie Wells was playing shortstop, Dick Seay was playing second base and Mule Suttles was playing first base. And that was the greatest! That was the million dollar infield right there. Couldn't nothing get through that infield. We could have played on any team in any league. That was the best team. We had one of the best ball teams ever. We were the only ones that was compared to the Homestead Grays."

The million dollar estimate of the infield's worth is modest compared to what their value would be today. Each member of the infield would command that much alone on the current player market. Their first year together, 1937, three-fourths of the infield was voted to the East squad in the annual all-star game. Only Dick Seay was passed over for a starting position. Homestead Grays' owner Cum Posey, who doubled as a writer for the Pittsburgh Courier, paid Ray the supreme compliment when the veteran baseball authority selected him to his annual All-America team as the best third baseman in black baseball for three consecutive years, 1936-1938. Obviously the 5' 7", 175 pounder stood tall in the eyes of Posey, who had seen virtually everyone who had played in the Negro Leagues since 1910.

A veritable human vacuum cleaner at third base, the right-handed swinger consistently hit over .300 and was a good baserunner. These

The 1937 East All-Star Team included Dandy (kneeling extreme left), Day (kneeling extreme right), and The Devil (kneeling third from left). Other players of note are Hall-of-Famer Buck Leonard (standing second from right), Mule Suttles (standing fourth from left), and Biz Mackey (standing sixth from left).

(Photo courtesy of Buck Leonard.)

qualities were also observed by Bill Klem, a National League umpire for 35 years, who regarded Dandridge as the best third baseman in baseball, black or white. Klem lauded Ray's ability to throw from any angle and to time his throws to make it easy on himself and still get his man. Other accolades from the arbiter acknowledged the superior gloveman as being "a terrific hitter" and running like "a jack rabbit on the bases". Ray's physical stature doesn't create the illusion of speed, but he was deceptively fast on the bases. Ray relates an incident while he was still a schoolboy that illustrates his swiftness afoot. "When I was in school I ran a 100-yard dash, fell down and got up and won the race. I guess I moved pretty good for my bowlegs," he laughs.

Willie Wells, Ray's sidekick at shortstop, was also bowlegged and fast on the bases. He was known as a battler and was not shy about going into a base with his spikes high. He was a superlative shortstop whose only shortcoming was the lack of a strong arm, which he compensated for with a quick release. And he also consistently hit over .300 with good extra base power. Ray regards the man that he played beside of both in the States and in Mexico as the best that he has ever seen. "I've seen two or three great shortstops. Lundy was good, but in my opinion Willie Wells was the best. The man didn't have a great arm but he'd throw out everybody. I think I seen Lloyd play. He was going out as I came in. And everybody used to talk about him. But Willie was still the best."

Dick Seay was a player much like an infielder of recent years, the Orioles' Mark Belanger. Seay had a golden glove but was weak at the plate. Ray has high praise for Seay's defensive abilities, "He was a hell of a fielder, one of the greatest second basemen fielding we ever had." Ray adds, "But he couldn't hit." Seay compensated for his lack of offensive punch by moving runners over in other ways. He was a good bunter, could execute the hit-and-run play and was a good baserunner.

But you don't have to be fast to be a good ballplayer. Mule Suttles wasn't fast on the bases and was awkward fielding the initial sack, "but he could hit the ball nine miles." The amiable big first sacker was known for being able to "hit them just as far as Josh Gibson" although he didn't hit them as often and was not as good a contact hitter as was Josh. Mule was a dangerous man to have to face in a pressure situation and his clutch home runs made him the hero in the all-star games of 1933 and 1935. Ray recalls once in Louisville when he saw Mule hit a ball over 500 feet only to have it caught.

When the Eagles needed another gold glove in the infield, they could call on Red Moore who often spiced up infield practice by taking the throws at first base behind his back. The Eagles also were afforded the luxury of having two quick catchers who were outstanding defensively.

The 1937 Newark Eagles featured the million dollar infield, consisting of first baseman Mule Suttles (standing second from right), second baseman Dick Seay (kneeling third from right), third baseman Ray Dandridge (kneeling extreme right), and shortstop Willie Wells (kneeling third from left). Also featured was ace pitcher Leon Day (kneeling fifth from left).

First they had Johnny Hayes behind the plate, and a year later Leon Ruffin joined the team. Ray regards both receivers highly but has added praise for Ruffin's throwing arm. "Ruffin couldn't hit a ball out of the infield but nobody ran on him," he emphasizes. "That's when we say we had a million dollar infield."

The superlative infield was complemented by good players at the other positions. "In the outfield we had Jimmy Crutchfield, Ed Stone, and Lennie Pearson. Later we had Johnny Davis and Monte Irvin when they came in. Back during that time these guys were rookies."

"Leon Day was with us. We played Day anywhere that we needed help. He was fast, he could hit, and he could throw." And, best of all, he could pitch. Day didn't lose a single league game during the 1937 season. "He wasn't very big but he was a great pitcher," Ray avows. "Nobody could throw any harder than he could." The Eagles also had Terris McDuffie pitching and, when he was right, he and Day formed a dynamic one-two punch for the Eagles.

Tex Burnett, the manager in 1937, had an easy time because he had so much outstanding talent on the team. "He didn't stay with us but one year," Ray remembers. "You know how it was years ago. Those guys weren't going to stay with you too long."

With Burnett's exit, former shortstop great Dick Lundy who had originally signed Ray for the Newark Dodgers, again took over the managerial reins. After a few years at the helm his legs were getting bad and he left the team to go back to Jacksonville to work as a redcap at the railroad station. Ray credits Lundy with being a major influence in his development as a fielder. In later years, while passing through Florida to play winter ball in the Caribbean, Ray would often stop and talk to his old mentor.

Following Lundy's departure, Willie Wells and Biz Mackey each managed the club. Ray recalls one particularly fond memory of Mackey. "One year Biz Mackey said, 'I'm not going to manage the East-West game unless you bring Dandridge to play third base for me.'" The East-West game was black baseball's most prestigious event, and players were honored to be selected. Mackey's feelings were representative of others who had managed the man with the velvet hands. They appreciated Ray because he always gave a hundred percent no matter who the manager was. "I ain't never had any trouble with a manager," Ray states emphatically. And managers didn't have any trouble making out the lineup with the million dollar infield around.

Unfortunately, that infield didn't remain intact over an extended period of time because, within a few years, the superstars on the left side of the infield, Ray Dandridge and Willie "Devil" Wells, departed for Mexico, and slick-fielding second sacker Dick Seay went to Puerto Rico.

◊   ◊   ◊

Ray still looks back on those days with the Eagles fondly, "Oh man, back during that time we didn't make any money but we had a lot of fun." When millionaire Mexican Jorge Pasquel came north looking for ballplayers for his team while passing out pesos like halloween candy, Ray found out that he could have a lot of fun and make some money, too.

That's when Dandridge, Day, and Wells jumped to Mexico along with some other black American baseball stars, including Josh Gibson. They went to Vera Cruz and won the pennant easily by thirteen games. Ray teamed with Wells to form a great keystone combination. In the field with the two bowlegged marvels on each side of the second sack, they looked like two sets of parentheses separated by a period.

In Mexico the money was good, the playing conditions were good, and more important, the living conditions were "beautiful, the most beautiful of all." Succumbing to the beauty of the land, Ray spent most of the next decade playing in Mexico, but he wasn't forgotten in the States. In 1941, although he was still in Mexico, Cum Posey again selected Dandridge on his All-America dream team. And Ray maintained a reciprocal interest in the States. On two separate occasions he returned to

Dandy and other Black Americans in Mexico.
Left to Right: Barney Brown, Josh Gibson, Ray Dandridge, Leroy Matlock,
Johnny Taylor and Bill Wright.
(Photo courtesy of Ray Dandridge.)

Newark briefly, but never stayed for more than one season before going
back to Pasquel's league.

The first time Ray returned stateside was in 1942. Hall-of-Famer
Monte Irvin, who later starred in the major leagues with the New York
Giants, considers that aggregation of playing talent to be the best in the
history of the Eagle organization, even superior to the championship club
of 1946 on which Irvin played. Unfortunately, the Manleys were either un-
willing or unable to retain the team intact. Bus Clarkson was traded to the
Philadelphia Stars, and Irvin and Dandridge opted for Mexico.

Ray credits the failure to hold the team together to Effa Manley, who
served as the business manager. "The only trouble we had was with Mrs.
Manley. She was the one who was pushy. You had to go see her if you
wanted anything. That was the reason a whole lot of players left," Ray explains. "That's why I left in 1940. I asked for a $25 raise, from $150 to
$175 a month." When Mrs. Manley refused to grant the small increase,
Ray and pitching star Leon Day caught a plane to Mexico together.

When Ray headed south of the Rio Grande again in mid-season of
1942, he was leading in the fans' balloting for the all-star team in the annual East-West classic. The only other time the star infielder returned to
the Eagles from his sojourn in Mexico was in 1944. "Well, I had been
playing in Mexico ever since 1940," he explains. "And then, in 1944, I
decided I wanted to stay in the States." Ray's return to Newark couldn't
have been a more productive year, as he hit .370, led the league in hits,
runs, and total bases, and again was voted to start the all-star game.

The game almost didn't come off that year, as the East squad held
out for more money. The owners, particularly Mrs. Manley, were irate.
But finally the management gave in and paid the players the $200 that
they had demanded. Ray responded to the increase in pay with three hits
in the all-star classic, albeit, in a losing cause. Certainly, if a most valuable player had been selected in the Negro National League that season,
the award would have gone to Ray Dandridge.

Despite his superlative season, Ray's tenure with the Manleys' team
was almost a duplicate of his previous stay; and at the end of the season
he went back to the Mexican league, this time as playing manager with
the Mexico City Reds. "I went over there with the money in my hand and
me and Mrs. Manley was negotiating for the contract," Ray declares, "and
I told her if she could match what Mexico was paying me to come to
Mexico, that I would stay. But she didn't agree on it, so I left and I went
back to Mexico. And I stayed there until around the end of 1948 and then
I came back to the States and I started playing with the New York Cubans
and that's when I was called in to go to tryout with Minneapolis back in
1949."

*Ray as a Newark Eagle in 1942 (top)
and at Ruppert Stadium in the late thirties (bottom).
(Photo courtesy of Ray Dandridge.)*

On one other occasion, because of a salary problem with Pasquel, Ray was ready to come back to the States but Pasquel had the militia stop him from boarding the train. "That was the incident during the time when the major leaguers were jumping," Ray explains, "and they were getting bonuses for coming down there. Some of them were getting $5,000 and some of them were getting $10,000 before they signed a contract. And back during that time they sent Ted Williams a blank check and told him to write in the amount if he wanted to come to Mexico."

"I had a good relationship with Pasquel. He was a very nice fellow and easy to get along with. The only thing we had trouble with was, he wouldn't give us bonuses when he did the major leaguers. During that time I went to Jorge and told him, 'Look, you're paying all of these ballplayers more money than you're paying us.' And I asked for more money and he said he couldn't give me no more money. So I told Pasquel I was leaving, and I packed up all my stuff and the kids and everything, and we were at the station ready to get on the train coming back to the United States. And then all of a sudden here comes a bunch of soldiers, and his secretary, and everybody. Pasquel had sent them. I was surprised to see them because I had my ticket and everything."

"And they held the train up. His secretary was in charge of everything, and he came back and said that Pasquel wanted to see me. And they say 'You can't leave now. Pasquel wants you back there.' I told them I wasn't going back. He said, 'You can't leave until you see Jorge. You'll have to come and talk to him.' I said, 'All right,' and agreed with it."

"He had the soldiers with him just to make sure that I wouldn't go out of Mexico City. Pasquel had that much authority. He was one of the biggest men down in Mexico at that time. He was one of the biggest millionaires."

"So I got off the train and they put me in a Cadillac, and drove me back, and took care of all the baggage. And I had to go back and negotiate, and that's when I got that raise in salary. Pasquel gave me a raise from $350 a month to $10,000 a year. And they got me another apartment with a maid, all our expenses were paid, and he gave me most everything. Everything was all right. I was Pasquel's number one boy! And then I started managing the team. He appointed me manager of the club at that time. Well, what can I say? I made more money in Mexico than I made most anywhere."

Ray always demonstrated a concern that players receive compensation commensurate with their talents. A few years later when Ray, as manager, needed a pitcher and a catcher, he came back to the states and signed former teammates Leon Day and Leon Ruffin. The arrangements had already been made in Mexico and Ray didn't waste any time. He told the two Eagles, "I'm going to give you the top notch price. If you want to go, we'll give you the money." Needless to say, both Eagles went with Ray to Mexico. This was right after Pasquel made his infamous raid on the major leagues, signing Sal Maglie, Max Lanier, Mickey Owen, and several others.

After the ban against the jumpers was lifted, Lanier and Maglie had successful major league careers, but Ray contends that "they were not any better than pitchers in our league. We had some pitchers who could really throw the ball." This was borne out by the fact that the major leaguers were outplayed by some of the Negro League veterans who were already there in Mexico.

When the major leaguers first arrived they were surprised to find players who were playing major league caliber baseball. On opening day Max Lanier, who had left a perfect 6-0 record and a 1.93 ERA with the St. Louis Cardinals when he jumped at Pasquel's money lure, opened on the mound for Mexico City against Ray's Vera Cruz team. Ray greeted him by blasting one of the southpaw's fastballs for a home run. Later in the game Lanier asked Dandridge and the other black American ballplayers, "Where did you guys come from?" "We came from the same place that you did," Ray responded, "from out of the United States." "Who in hell are you?," Lanier retorted. "I never heard of any of you guys before." "Well, we've been here," Ray answered, "We've just been waiting for you to get here."

The former Cardinal hurler did more than just talk to Ray. After the home run, he knocked him down the next time he came to bat, and routinely "gave him a shave" thereafter. Ray also played against Lanier in the Caribbean. He recalls that Lanier would always throw at him just as he had done in Mexico. While both of the former players were participating in an old-timers game in Miami 35 years later, Ray asked Lanier about the knockdown pitches. "I said, 'Max, answer me a question. Why did you throw at me when we were in Mexico?' He said, 'The manager told me to throw at you. I had orders.'" Lanier's manager was Adolph Luque, who's characterized by Tommy LaSorda as "a tough S.O.B."

Luque characterized the Latin temperaments that led to frequent flare-ups on the field of play. Players couldn't allow themselves to be intimidated if they were going to play in the Latin leagues. Not only were batters frequently knocked down by pitchers, but baserunners also would cut an infielder without any qualms. Sometimes there were pay-backs for something that had happened earlier in the States.

Ray was on the delivering end in one such pay-back. The initial incident occurred when Roy Campanella, playing with the Baltimore Elite

Giants, cut Ray in a play at third base. Ray calls it "just one of those things". "I wasn't expecting it", he says "but I told him, 'Well, I'll get you one day, or bust'".

Ray didn't have to bust. All he had to do was bide his time, and one winter at Tropical Stadium in Havana, Cuba the scenario was complete for a pay-back. His team was playing Campy's team. "He cut me once and quite a bit after that I had my chance and I got even," Ray remembers. "I was on second base and a guy hit a line drive to center field and I was rounding third base and the man had me out by about eight feet. He had me completely out. It came to me all of a sudden because I knew they had me out. I was flying around there and I hollered, 'I've got you now! I've got you now!' And then I jumped in the air. I guess you know I went in safe. I looked and Campanella was almost up in the stands. I didn't hit him because he had already got out of the way." Afterwards Campanella "didn't say nothing," because "he knew I was going to get even with him. That was the end of it. I forgot about it a long time ago."

Campy may have forgotten the incident too, but he hasn't forgotten the man. Over forty years later, at Dodgertown in spring training, he greeted Ray warmly. "Hello, Squatty," he said, using Ray's old nickname from the Negro Leagues and obviously pleased to see his old adversary. A member of the Veteran's committee for the Hall of Fame, Campanella told his attendant Sam that he was going to try to help Ray get elected. "I saw him play," the Dodger great said. "He was that good. He deserves it." Campy had always been an admirer of Ray's talents. "I played against Ray Dandridge and I never saw anyone better as a fielder or runner," he remembered, "and he hit well over .300".

Campanella was not the only Hall of Fame catcher to slide into Ray with harmful intent. In Akron, Ohio the great Josh Gibson cut Ray's uniform off in a play at third base. Josh had smashed a double and was trying to stretch it into a triple. The throw came in and Ray had him trapped but the big burly Gibson kept running and came in with his spikes high. "He jumped right straight in the air and into my arms. He cut me on the arm and tore up my uniform in the front, but I got him out," Ray declares. "Back during that time if you didn't get out of their way, they'd cut you. I didn't pay it no mind. I said to him, 'I thought we were friends.'"

They were friends off the field and were to be teammates a few years afterwards in Mexico. But their friendship did not develop into a close personal relationship. "I never hung out with him," Ray explains. "One time we had to stop Josh from dropping his wife from the second floor in Mexico. His wife screamed 'bloody murder'". Gibson's behavior in Mexico was symptomatic of a greater underlying problem which subsequently manifested itself. "A few years later Josh had a nervous break-down," Ray adds sadly. But Ray doesn't like to dwell on that part of the big slugger's life, preferring the positive memories. "He was the one catcher that we had who was better than anybody the major leagues had. Nobody hit the ball better than Josh Gibson. I'll tell you the truth, Josh wasn't no great *catcher*," he says, while emphasizing that Gibson's forte was pounding the horsehide. "Josh Gibson was a great hitter. That man could hit! I've seen him. I played with him and I've played against him. If the shortstop was standing still and that man hit a ball and no farther than a step away, the shortstop couldn't hardly move to get to the ball because it was hit so hard that it was already by him. A whole lot of times I've seen that. I saw him in Comiskey Park, in an all-star game, hit a ball in a microphone. It was a dead line drive too. That man was a great hitter. None was better."

After two years in Mexico Josh returned to the States but Ray chose to remain in Mexico. During his stay there Ray played on an all-star team with future Yankee great and current Hall-of-Famer Whitey Ford. Ray and Whitey managed the American ballplayers against the native Mexican players.

Ray always had good success batting against Whitey, a practice that continued when Ray was at Minneapolis and Whitey was with the Yankee farm club at Kansas City. Diminutive pitcher Dave Barnhill, Ray's team-mate at Minneapolis, expressed this ability from his vantage point, "Ray Dandridge hit Whitey Ford like he was his son." Reminiscing, Barnhill continued, "When Kansas City came to Minneapolis he would say, 'Who's pitching?' Dandridge would just smile soon as he saw Whitey walk out there. And he hit him that day just like he owned him."

Whitey Ford was not the only Yankee great that Ray played against. In the spring of 1947 the Yankees played a series in Caracas against the local teams. "They came through Venezuela in spring training," Ray remembers. "They went from spring training camp and they were touring all through the Latin countries. And the Latin countries called and we made up an all-star team of Cuban and American ballplayers and such. And I was picked as one of the American ballplayers to go down there and play that year." Ray played at second base with Luis Aparicio's father on his right side at shortstop.

Bill Bevans, who was to have a fall flirtation with immortality before both the courtship and his World Series no-hitter was broken-up by one swing of Cookie Lavagetto's bat in the ninth inning; and Allie Reynolds, who was also to have a fling with fame by hurling two no-hitters in 1951, were the Yankee hurlers that day.

Ray doesn't remember the pitchers because "back during that time I didn't know too many Yankee ballplayers. I knew Phil Rizzuto was on the team, and Yogi Berra was on the team because Yogi is the one who missed the ball and we won by one run."

Ray went down with a contract to play one game but after his first stellar performance, they quickly made financial arrangements for him to play the other games in the series. Many baseball observers were surprised that the black aggregation defeated the powerful Yankees, who were to go on to a pennant and World Series victory over the Dodgers that fall.

However, the black players themselves were not surprised. The players in the Negro Leagues always knew that they could have played in the major leagues if they had been given the opportunity. "If you would pick an all-star team of the black leagues to play white teams during that time, we could have beat them," Ray says. "We would! I don't think we would have looked back. We could have won walking away. I'm talking about an all-star team. If you took one of our teams intact into the majors, I don't know what would have happened. In a way we would have been a little rough in some spots on these teams where the white teams would be strong."

"You've got to have your best pitchers. We had about four. Then the other men were in-and-out. Sometimes in the Negro Leagues we had a combination of weak hitters. But the other men were holding them up because they were good fielders, but not the type of hitters that we wanted. Maybe we had a catcher who couldn't hit a ball out of the infield or a shortstop who couldn't hit. Now the major leaguers may have a catcher who could pepper that ball."

What would have happened in that event is pure speculation. What is fact, however, is that some of the greatest players in the great American pastime played out their entire careers without ever having the opportunity to compete in the major leagues. Ray Dandridge is one of these men.

◊   ◊   ◊

After he retired from the game for good, Ray still had a family to support, but his entire life had been spent playing baseball and he didn't have an alternate career to fall back on. Willing to work at whatever kind of work he could find, he soon found a benefactor. "After I quit baseball I started tending bar," Ray says of finding his niche for a second career. "A Jewish fellow in Newark, Harry Weinstein, wanted me to help him out with his bar. I didn't know that much about it but I started tending bar and he made me manager of the place in a few weeks. It was called Dave's Long Bar. I stayed with that man for 18 years."

Often patrons, not knowing Ray's identity, would engage in a discussion about who was the greatest third baseman of all time. Being a good listener is an acquired characteristic of a bartender, so while these arguments continued, Ray just listened and didn't say anything. But he knew the answer. And so did anyone else who had ever seen him play. But no one asked him, and the unrecognized bartender sat quietly at the end of the bar and just listened.

Ray enjoyed his work there and after the owner sold that establishment, he bought another bar in Orange. "Then," says Ray, "he sold it and went into the liquor store business and I went along with him as manager of the liquor store. Then he died and his wife took over and sold it."

After that Ray put in a brief stint at the Peppermint lounge, but "it didn't work out. It was a small place at that time and I didn't last a year there," he recalls. "During that time is when I left and went to the recreation department."

Ray remained with Newark's recreation department for eight years, working with the city's youth. "A lot of good kids are strayed by a few who aren't good" he says. "I tried to help them as much as I could to get them off on the right foot."

Insight gained from Ray's seven decades of experience forms the basis for the advice that he passes on to youngsters who want to achieve success on the baseball diamond. "To be a good ballplayer, a man's got to have it inside of him. He just wants to do it," he tells aspiring ballplayers. "If you've got it inside of you and you want to do it, and if you've got just a little ability about yourself, you can do it."

"Just keep hustling," he admonishes young athletes, "and they've got to take you." Sometimes Ray is a bit wistful when he talks to youngsters who have the chance at the major leagues that was denied him. As a youth the color of his skin prevented him from reaching the apex of professional baseball, but today's youngsters are limited only by their own ability and determination. "I didn't go all the way," he explains, "but that doesn't mean that they can't."

The current generation of black major leaguers have never had to face the frustrations that Ray's generation encountered. However, unlike many old-time ballplayers, Ray doesn't denigrate the present day players. According to him, many modern players are as good as those of his day. "A whole lot of today's players could hit during the time that I was playing. A hitter is going to hit a left-hander or a right-hander. If you are a major league ballplayer, I believe that you can hit a right-hander the same as a left-hander. Just like all these guys that are making all this money. They have to play every game. They see a ball, they swing."

"But ballplayers today are different in many ways. Like the strike. In a way the boys are trying to get something for themselves. The way things are going nowadays, I say more power to the ballplayers." Contemporary players are reaping the benefits from the groundwork laid by players from an earlier generation. Not only financially, but in other ways as well. This is especially true of the current black players.

"A whole lot of black ballplayers should appreciate the old-timers," Ray says. "They don't even think there were any old-timers. They don't even think about it. I mean back during the time when you had to go on your own. These old-timers are the ones who were fighting back during the time before the line was broken. They don't even think about it. And I don't think it's right. Some of these black ballplayers are making good money. Now at least these guys could make it so the old-timers from the Negro Leagues could have a gathering every year. I would like to see those reunions go on, so these old ballplayers could at least meet once a year."

For awhile there was an opportunity for the old-time Negro Leaguers to get together. Beginning in 1979, there was an annual reunion in Kentucky. Ray was one of the small group of former players invited to the initial get-together, which was organized as a surprise 83rd birthday party honoring Negro League great Clint Thomas.

"Now this thing started from a young preacher," Ray explains. "They invited about 12 of us ballplayers to Greenup, Kentucky." The players didn't know what to expect from a small southern town off the beaten path that had no connection with black baseball. "When we first went out there we were surprised ourselves. And you know good and well back during that time years ago, you couldn't even hardly put a foot in Kentucky unless something happened."

The next year the reunion expanded and became a part of the Tri-State Regatta held in neighboring Ashland, Kentucky, where they also organized what was hoped to become the black equivalent of Cooperstown's Baseball Museum. "This was what they called the Black Baseball Hall of History," Ray continues. "And every year for quite a few years ballplayers were coming back to these reunions. It started out with just a few and they wound up with about 60 ballplayers out there each year. I don't know if they're going to ever have it again because of a lack of funds."

The former players appreciated the opportunity to get together, and could not say enough good things about the people who made it possible. Ray expresses the feelings of all the players. "I think those people at Ashland are the greatest people I've ever seen. Those people treated us like we were a bunch of kings. And right now if anybody says anything against Kentucky, I'll give them a big argument."

While the modern black ballplayers have failed to recognize and publicly acknowledge the contributions made by the veterans of the Negro Leagues, the civic leaders of an older generation fully understand how valuable those contributions were to the achievement of the current conditions for blacks, both on the athletic fields and in society.

On August 14, 1980, Ray was honored by The Newark City Council when they presented him with a resolution for his service to "all the kids that he has touched" as a supervisor of public works. The proclamation was presented with "respect and appreciation . . . for the enormous success he achieved as a professional baseball player and . . . the immeasurable contribution he made as a pioneer in breaking down racial barriers for the many black athletes who followed in his footsteps."

Ray was grateful to the City Council for their recognition. His ties to the City went far beyond the bounds of baseball. It was his home. He first came to Newark in 1934 and lived in the same house for over 40 years. Ray bought the house with $7500 of the $10,000 bonus that Jorge Pasquel's brother gave him for going to Mexico in 1940. It was in this house that Ray reared his daughter and two sons. "All my family is right around here. Everybody I know is here," Ray said a few years prior to his decision to leave Newark and move to the Sunshine State. "I've got nineteen grandchildren and five great-grandchildren. But none of them are ballplayers yet," Ray laughs. "That's a funny thing. They all like to come here on weekends. You ought to see this place when they all get here. I'm the Godfather!"

Ray left behind a lifetime of memories when he opted for the warmer climate and lifestyle of a Florida retiree. But not all of Ray's memories of Newark were pleasant. "They broke into my house and stole most of my trophies. Some nice ones. I used to have trophies all lined across the mantle. But someone took them all. The police never caught them. People asked me 'Why don't you move? This is the ghetto, you know.'" But Ray didn't leave. "Nobody's going to run me out," he responded. "They don't mess with me. When I go outside, it's 'Hello, Mr. Dandridge'." Even the hoods who were the ones most likely responsible for burglarizing his home spoke circumspectly when he was around.

In the wake of this incident Ray still remained in his adopted hometown until after his retirement when he and his wife, Henrietta, bought a home in the growing community of Palm Bay, Florida. On the way down to his new home Ray stopped by his childhood home but found things had changed. "I went through Richmond when I went to Florida and I didn't see a living human being that I know," he relates.

From Richmond to Newark to Florida, by way of the Western Hemisphere. That's the route that Ray took from the beginning to the present.
Relaxing in retirement now, Ray has mellowed somewhat and, although
disappointed, he didn't get upset when he narrowly missed selection to
the Hall of Fame for the third consecutive year.

Although it appears that the Hall of Fame may have forgotten Ray,
those who know him have not. After living fifty years in Newark's central
ward, Ray likes to go back occasionally to "make the rounds" at the Cozy
Corner, Hooker's Elbow Room, and other favorite establishments where
he "raps with the guys". Recently he returned to his adopted hometown
where he was honored by having a ballpark named after him. On Wednesday, July 25, 1985 a ball field in Newark's Westside Park was renamed
The Raymond E. Dandridge, Sr. Baseball Field. The honor carried a special significance because Ray used to practice on this same field in his earlier years. When the dedication was read at the ceremonies, he received a
standing ovation. Not one for formal speeches, Ray summed up his feelings quite simply. "It is a great honor," he said sincerely. "Thank you all.
I love you."

Ray doesn't like to talk about himself, preferring to let his records
speak for him. "I set a record most every place I've ever been and my
name is in the record books of those countries for playing baseball. And it
never swelled my head. My records stand and I figure if anything can be
done, look up the record." Casey Stengel couldn't have phrased it any better. "And right now I get fan mail from all over the United States. I'm
more popular today than I've ever been."

But the record books only tell part of the story. Off the field Ray was
always himself, taking life where he could find it and living it to the hilt.
"I've had good experiences in life and I've enjoyed it too," Ray says.
"Most everywhere I've been, they have treated me nice."

While the retired warrior displays a reserved resignation to past
things that were beyond his control, there are no regrets about the things
that he could control. In what could be a personal denouement Ray concludes, "And if I had it to do over again, I'd do it again the same way. I
wish I could live it all over again."

"I loved the game."

◊   ◊   ◊

No eloquent eulogy could better capture the character of the man than
those four words. When the Hall of Fame's Special Committee on Negro
League players was formed in 1971, this special essence was recognized
when Ray was among the top five players nominated. Satchel Paige was
the committee's first selection and after the induction ceremonies that

year, Ray said "Satchel deserved it. I'm hoping I'll be the next one." But 15 years have come and gone, ten players from the Negro Leagues have been inducted into the Hall of Fame, the special committee has been disbanded, and Ray is still on the outside looking in. He has been disillusioned for so long that he no longer is affected by the near misses. "I was one of the top five when they first took somebody in," he says in resignation, "and I'm still not in there."

When the special committee on Negro League players was disbanded, it put the other deserving Negro League players at a disadvantage because they were forced to be considered by the regular Veterans Committee which is limited to only two selections per year. And many of the committee members never saw the Negro League players. "I don't see why they cut the special committee out," Ray says. "If they're trying to bring it back in, it would be nice. There's quite a few more players from the Negro Leagues who deserve to be in the Hall of Fame."

Once the door to the major leagues was opened to black players, Ray's goal was to make it all the way to the top in spite of his age. "That's the reason why I kept playing as long as I did. I thought maybe I could make it. I could die happy if I could just have played one day in the major leagues." But he was denied that privilege because of a circumstance of birth. Now it's the same situation with the Hall of Fame. But Ray refuses to get his hopes up. He has been disappointed too many times. Stoically Ray says, "If it happens, it happens." All of the hardships and injustices of the past would have been worth the sacrifice if he was just able to share that honor with the other greats of his generation. "All ballplayers want to go into the Hall of Fame," Ray admits. "A man would like to see these things when he is living. Now what good is it going to do me when they're putting me under the ground?" After last year's near miss, one member of the veteran's committee said that all Ray had to do to be elected was to "stay alive for another year."

He has done that—and everything else that was humanly possible to demonstrate his credentials for the Hall of Fame. After the Ashland Hall of History closed down, the memorabilia was sold to the National Baseball Hall of Fame and Museum. So now Ray's uniform from Mexico City is on display in Cooperstown, the baseball Mecca. But until his likeness in bronze is included alongside those of the other greats in the marbled halls adjoining the museum, the Hall of Fame will be incomplete.

The appropriate recognition is long overdue and when the honor does come, it will be as Ray envisioned the occasion fifteen years earlier when it first became a possibility.

"It will be a beautiful thing!"

DAY

"If we had one game to win, we wanted Leon to pitch."
                                                    Monte Irvin

LEON DAY

The best pitcher in the Negro National League during the last fifteen years of it's existence was a slender, right-hander with a blinding fastball. His name was Day, but he was the color of night.

I had the pleasure of meeting the former pitching ace a half-dozen summers ago while trekking up the Atlantic seaboard in search of veterans from the Negro Leagues. When I arrived at his home on Harlem Avenue in Baltimore, Leon greeted me in his bathrobe and proved to be a gracious host. I spent an enjoyable afternoon in his living room listening to stories about the players from the Negro leagues. As is his manner, he talked more about others than about himself.

Leon is soft spoken, and has a quick wit and charming sense of humor. The next stop on my itinerary was with Bill Harvey, a left-handed pitcher who played with the Pittsburgh Crawfords and Baltimore Elite Giants. Day called to tell him that I was on my way over. "There's a man here looking for you from the I.R.S.," he deadpanned, getting a good chuckle from Harvey's reaction before finally telling his former teammate the real purpose of his call. After hanging up the phone, he laughed and said, "Harvey's older than a New Guinea coconut tree. And they have to be 100 years old before they bear coconuts."

I've talked with Leon several times since, at the Negro League reunions and more recently, when he visited Ray Dandridge in Florida. At the reunions, an observer would never have guessed that this quiet, fun-loving fellow had been one of the best pitchers in the country when in his prime. Leon is unpretentious and genuinely unaffected by his past accomplishments. He is satisfied to sit quietly outside the spotlight and let someone else hold center stage. Only rarely, unless responding to a direct question, will he relate an on-the-diamond experience because that would *be too much like bragging. His modesty belies the great player that he truly was.*

Day was the Newark Eagles' ace moundsman and delighted in hooking up with Satchel Paige in pitching duels. Monte Irvin speaks for the Negro League veterans when he discusses these match-ups and the merits of his former teammate. "One day we were playing against Satchel Paige and Leon said, 'Get me a run.' But Satchel had us shut out, and Leon hit a home run that won the game. That's the kind of player he was."

"If you could have seen this man when he was in his prime," Monte marvels. "Leon Day was probably the finest all around player I've ever seen. He was a good pitcher, had the heart of a lion, and a real good fastball. He threw as hard as Bob Gibson. And he had a small but good curve, and had control of it. He could field his position, he was a good hitter, he could outrun me, he played second base, and played a great outfield."

"When the going got tough you wanted Leon Day on your side." Monte alludes to Mets' superstar Dwight Gooden in describing Day. "If Dwight Gooden continues to pitch the way he has, he may become the kind of pitcher that Leon Day was. We always said that if we had one game to win, we wanted Leon to pitch. I'm proud of having known Leon Day."

During a twenty-two year career played in a half-dozen countries, winter and summer, Leon just did his job and didn't let anything bother him too much. During that span the right-hander pitched in more games than he can remember. "A lot of that stuff I've forgotten," he says. "I can't remember all of that." Remembering the good times and not worrying about the bad times—that's Leon's way. He fends off queries about specific games with characteristic humor, "Please don't start me to lying," he laughs.

One thing that Leon does remember quite well is the color barrier that prevented so many talented players from starring in the major league. But the memory leaves no residue of bitterness. "I never resented not having the opportunity to play in the major leagues," he says. "I have no regrets. I was happy for Robinson and Doby. It was good that some of the younger players got a chance. I was glad to see us finally make it."

He was equally pleased for the Negro League veterans who were selected for the Hall of Fame when that door was belatedly opened to black players from his generation.

That's Leon Day.

"He was a sweetheart," said Dave Barnhill, who battled him on the mound more times than either of them cared to remember. "He was a real Prince," adds shortstop great Willie Wells, who saw all the players in both the East and the West from 1925 through 1950.

That's also Leon Day.

Satchel Paige is known by virtually everyone, even those who are not generally baseball fans. In addition to being one of the greatest pitchers who ever lived, he was a charmer and a master showman whose flamboyance and braggadocio attracted crowds everywhere he went.

Frequently while traveling across the country playing all comers, Paige would call in his outfielders and strike out the side. Naturally, the media feasted on each incident, spreading his name coast-to-coast and even overseas. The tall, lanky right-hander, who called his pea-sized fastball the "bee-ball" because it hummed, was known worldwide.

But during the years when Satchel's colorful antics were entertaining the crowds and making him a legend in his own lifetime, there was also another outstanding pitcher performing beyond the periphery of organized baseball in the shadowy world of the Negro Leagues. While Satchel was the king-pin of the Negro American League in the West, Leon Day was his eastern counterpart in the Negro National League.

Contrasting with Satchel, Leon was quiet, soft-spoken, and modest. In his prime he was the best pitcher in the Negro National League, but his name and exploits are known only to those players who played against him, and those baseball scholars who have delved into the miasmic segment of baseball research that is the history of the Negro Leagues.

Even today Leon Day will not toot his own horn, but the voices of those veterans of the Negro Leagues who are still living speak for him, and his records speak for themselves.

Many former players compare his fastball with that of Bob Gibson. Others say that while his fastball may have had less velocity, it was "sneaky" and more effective than Gibson's. Monte Irvin, a former teammate of Day's, indicates that Leon was a little better pitcher than the Hall of Fame hurler of more recent vintage.

Black baseball's big event was their annual East-West all-star game, which brought together the greats of both Negro leagues into one showcase. In the spotlight of this spectacle Satchel Paige, because of his reputation and colorful exploits, often held center stage. Five times he appeared in the mid-season classic and, pitching against the opposing league's best hitters, struck out a total of 13 batters. Viewed in context of the opposition, these were truly outstanding accomplishments. But, as great as his performances were, they only placed Satchel in the number two position in each category. The record holder in both instances is Leon Day, who amassed 14 strikeouts in six all-star games. Day's all-star records would have been even more impressive had he not missed four prime seasons due to a variety of circumstances, which included military service in World War II, two arm injuries, and a jump to the Mexican League.

In accumulating these statistical records, the little right-hander with the sneaky fastball and sharp-breaking curve performed feats that outshone his flashy, and more famous contemporary.

The 1942 East-West game was a classic example. The newspapers had headlined a head-to-head match-up between Satchel and Leon, who were slated to start on the mound for their respective leagues. The Chicago Defender, one of the two leading black newspapers, boldly proclaimed "Paige versus Day Sunday," but as events unfolded, neither of the league aces were on the rubber when the game began.

Satchel had been embroiled in controversy over newspaper accounts concerning his recent comments that the major leagues couldn't pay him enough money to play for them. In the eyes of many blacks his statements were detrimental to the eventual entry of black players into the major leagues, and Satchel's image was to some degree tarnished by his remarks.

The black public wanted to hear what Satchel had to say about the media's reports. So after six innings of play with the score tied, the umpires held up the game while Satchel addressed the fans over the stadium's public address system to tell his side of the issue. Comiskey Park's 48,000 fans and players from both dugouts listened intently as the

Leon Day, short-arming his sneaky fastball. In 1942, Day struck out 18 batters in a single game to establish a Negro League record.

baseball idol denied the statements attributed to him by the newspapers. He said that he had been misquoted on almost everything and assured all those present, "I want you to know that I did not say anything against the use of Negro players in the big leagues."

After his unprecedented speech to the fans, Satchel received a thunderous ovation as he took the field to begin the seventh inning. His appearance was viewed as a sign that the West was going to lock up the victory, having saved their best hurler for the last three innings. But the presumed hero-to-be gave up a run to the East team in their half of the seventh inning before he could retire the side. As though to atone for his sin of allowing a run, Satchel singled to start a West rally in their half of the seventh frame. Hall-of-Famer Cool Papa Bell followed with another hit, moving the tying run into scoring position.

The East squad's manager, Vic Harris, didn't want to chance losing the game, and called time-out to confer with his coach, Tex Burnette of the New York Black Yankees. With the outcome of the game hanging in the balance, the East skipper looked to the bullpen in right-field where Leon was warming up and called on the Newark ace to save the day for his team.

The scenario was complete for Leon to enact what was probably his most superb performance. Entering the game in the seventh inning with two outs and the tying and go-ahead runs on base, he promptly retired the first batter on a ground ball to shortstop Willie Wells to squelch the West squad's rally.

Then over the remaining two innings Leon struck out five of the six batters that he faced, the last four in succession. Only clean-up hitter Willard Brown even touched the ball, fouling out to catcher Josh Gibson. Leon recalls that he pitched "high and tight" to the ever-dangerous Brown, who is classed by Tommy LaSorda as the greatest hitter to never play in the major leagues (excluding a cup of coffee with the St. Louis Browns in 1947). The other West all-stars took their cuts at Day's fastball and hit nothing but air.

In the major league all-star game of 1934, Carl Hubbell had become a baseball immortal by striking out five consecutive American League stars. What is often overlooked in this extraordinary feat is that Hubbell faced a total of 13 men and gave up two hits and two walks during his historic stint.

But in Day's superlative outing, of the seven batters that he faced, he struck out five and did not allow a baserunner. Only the end of the game prevented him from extending his strike-out streak. Leon was just warming to the task and had obligingly struck out the side in the bottom half of the ninth inning to seal the 5-2 East victory.

*In the 1942 All-Star Game, Day faced seven batters and fanned five of
them—the last four in succession to end the game.*

The 1942 season was truly sensational for Leon. Only three weeks earlier in a night game against the pennant-contending Baltimore Elite Giants, he had struck out 18 batters to establish a league record, while fashioning a one-hit masterpiece. The only hit was a bloop single by Pee Wee Butts to open the game.

Leon has forgotten many of the games that he pitched over the years, but even today he still recalls this one. "Pee Wee Butts, the lead-off batter, was a right-handed hitter and I threw him a fastball in on his fists. He hit it on the handle right over the shortstop's head into left field. It was a little blooper, like a dying quail. That was the only hit they got." Thereafter Baltimore's big hitters were stymied as Leon smoked them with his fastball. "They had a good team and had some good hitters," Leon observes. "The ones I was most worried about were Bill Wright, Henry Kimbro and Sammy T. Hughes." Among the batters that he victimized was the Elite's young catcher, future Hall-of-Famer Roy Campanella. "They had Campanella over there," Leon continues, "and I just threw fastballs by him. I had 18 strikeouts and he was three of them."

The Elites were locked in a nip-and-tuck struggle for the pennant with the Homestead Grays, who were precariously holding on to the league lead. The battle went down to the final day of the season, with the Grays playing Day's Newark Eagles a double-header and still needing one victory to clinch the flag.

Controversy raged as the Eagles manager, Willie Wells, withheld his ace moundsman from the decisive game and started young Harry Hopgood instead. The game was played at Ebbetts Field and Leon started in the center pasture, batted second in the lineup and had one of the Eagles' four hits. Baltimore partisans considered Leon's absence from the mound to be an ill-disguised effort to hand the pennant to the Grays on a silver platter. Whatever the reason for the maneuver, the Eagles lost without him on the mound, thus defaulting the league crown to the Homestead Grays.

After the Eagles' regular season ended Leon went back home, but when the Grays dropped their first three world series games to the Kansas City Monarchs, Newark owner, Abe Manley, was contacted by Cum Posey, who wanted Leon to play with his Grays for the remainder of the series.

Although modest to a fault, Leon is equally honest when responding to the question of why the Grays chose him. "I guess they picked me to go against Satchel because they figured I could beat him."

When told by Manley of Posey's request, Leon quickly agreed. "I liked to throw against Satchel," he says. "I was looking forward to pitching against him. I had pitched against him before down in Puerto Rico one winter. I think it was '39. He was on the best team on the island and I was playing with the worst team. In the ninth inning, we had two outs and I had him beat by one run. They had men on second and third and the ball was hit to the first baseman, who was right by first base. When the catcher, Johnny Hayes, saw him field the ball he just knew he was going over and touch the bag because there were two outs already. So the catcher turned around and walked on away, walking back to the third base dugout with his back turned to the field. And you know the first baseman, a Puerto Rican that we called Suscio, threw that ball to him. And he's got his back turned! Two men scored on that play to give them the game. And I had him *beat!"*

So the stage was set for a rematch. The Grays picked up Leon and three other players in Newark and they proceeded by bus to Kansas City, where the Monarchs were planning to wrap up the world championship in front of the hometown fans. Naturally, their colorful star, the fabulous Satchel Paige, was going to start on the mound in what was expected to be the final game of the series. But the Kansas City brain trust had not counted on what the Grays had planned for them. The Monarch players were so confident that most of them didn't care who the Grays pitched, and the owners allegedly gave their approval for the Grays to use Leon and the other players. Evidently they thought that with Satchel toeing the rubber, it didn't matter who the Grays pitched.

The Monarchs' clean-up hitter, slugger Willard Brown, perhaps best summarized the team's sentiments when he expressed his own, "I didn't care who they pitched. I just knew whoever it was, he had to throw the ball over the plate. And if he did I was going to hit it." But then Willard was the kind of hitter who didn't care if the sun didn't shine—just as long as someone would hold a lantern for him so he could see the ball.

Perhaps Kansas City should have remembered the East-West game and how Leon had struck out the Monarchs' best hitters and pinned the loss on Satchel. If they did remember that outing, no doubt they had a feeling of deja vu when the game ended. Not only had Leon won the game 4-1, while striking out 12 men and yielding only 1 walk and 5 hits, but the slender hurler also had a double off Satchel when on the other end of the pitcher-batter confrontation. Whatever lack of concern that the Monarchs had prior to the game quickly disappeared in the wake of Day's sterling performance.

Looking back four-and-a-half decades later, Leon assesses the Monarch hitters that he faced in that world series. "Buck O'Neil and Willard Brown were pretty tough. I tried to pitch O'Neil outside and he hit the ball, and I tried to go inside on him and he hit the ball. He was a little tough on me. Later on I met Brown in the service and we played together.

Joe Greene and Ted Strong didn't give me any trouble. Greene had been in our league for awhile before he went to the Monarchs and Strong didn't have a real good eye at the plate, but if he hit it you were in trouble."

The Monarchs' inability to make contact off his deliveries resulted in thirteen baseballs being thrown out of play by umpires Billy Donaldson and Bullet Rogan amid allegations of cutting the ball, to which the usually easy-going pitcher bristles and says, "I never cut a ball in my life! The only thing I cut was the bat out of their hands."

Refuted in their claim, the Monarch management focused on a clearer issue, the use of the four ringers. In addition to Day, the Grays had used his Eagle teammates Lennie Pearson and Eddie Stone, as well as Bus Clarkson from the Philadelphia Stars. The Monarchs' co-owner, Tom Baird, protested the game, disclaiming the approval that the Grays' contended was given.

The outcry started almost immediately after the last pitch was thrown. "I beat Satchel out there in Kansas City," Leon recalls, "and after I beat him they had an argument about it. We were supposed to go to Philadelphia to play the next game but they said that they weren't going to let me play with them anymore."

Following the game, the teams' executives had met and issued a ruling in which the protest was upheld, the four borrowed players were declared ineligible and the victory was disallowed. "They took the game away from us," Leon declares. After the ruling that they could not continue to play with the Grays, the four affected players returned home on a train. "They paid for the train ride home," Leon explains. "We always got our transportation."

Transportation was not all that he players in question received for their performance. Although they were on salary with their own teams and weren't promised any money when recruited to play with the Grays, there was an extra bonus. "Cum Posey came up to me after the game and gave me $100 out of his own pocket," Leon remembers, "because I beat Satchel. The others probably got something, but I don't know. I didn't see them get paid." When asked if he thought that he would have been paid if he had lost the game to Satchel, the soft-spoken star laughingly surmised, "Probably, since they had a good crowd." While the crowd did provide a good payday for the management, the game did not provide the victory that the hometown crowd came to see. But without Leon on the mound, the Monarchs were able to wrap up the championship the next day.

At the conclusion of post-season play, Grays' owner Cum Posey, who doubled as a columnist for the *Pittsburgh Courier,* selected his annual All-American Team for the Negro Leagues. His two pitchers were

The 1942 Newark Eagles pitching corps. Leon Day is third from the left. Only his brilliant pitching kept the team in the scramble for the flag. (Photo courtesy of Larry Hogan.)

Leon Day and Satchel Paige, with Leon being rated over Satchel. Posey wrote, "Leon Day was the best pitcher in Negro Baseball . . . despite the fact that he was used daily, either as a pitcher, outfielder, or infielder." Besides what Leon did in the all-star game and in the world series, Posey's evaluation was in recognition of what Day had done to Cum's powerful Grays during the regular season.

67

During the first weekend of July, with the front running Grays riding high, the Eagles had beaten them three games and tied the remaining one in back-to-back double-headers. While pitching and hitting sixth in the batting order, Leon had defeated them 6-2 in the opener at Pittsburgh's Forbes Field on Saturday. The next day at Washington's Griffith Stadium, while playing left field, Leon and Willie Wells had back-to-back doubles in the 14th inning to give the Eagles a 6-5 victory. That smash was only one of the three hits that he collected for the game.

Leon was always tough on the Grays. He had beaten them so much they would frequently save their ace, Raymond Brown, for the second game of a doubleheader rather than have him go head-to-head against Day.

Their respect for his pitching talent was shared by the entire league. In mid-August there was much talk about the Pittsburgh Pirates giving tryouts to some black players. Although the offer was later retracted, Leon was one of the four players selected by the *Pittsburgh Courier* for the honor. "Leon Day is the type of hurler the Pirates need," the *Courier* stated. "He has all the qualities necessary for the majors. We believe he could do much better than the Pirates' leading hurler, Rip Sewell." The needs of the Pirates were considered by the newspaper when making their choices, with the other selectees being Willie Wells, Josh Gibson, and Sam Bankhead.

◊   ◊   ◊

Winning awards and honors such as these, striking out 18 batters while spinning a one-hit gem, saving the all-star game by retiring all seven batters that he faced, including five by strikeouts (the last four in succession to end the game), and besting Satchel Paige in the World Series while striking out another dozen batters—to most it would seem like a herculean year, but not to the one who accomplished all this. "Oh, yeah, that was a good year," Leon states matter-of-factly, "but I've had better years."

"I think my best year was 1937," he declares. "I don't know how many games I won but I only lost one. "And that game was only an exhibition! In league play, he finished the 61-game season with an unblemished 13-0 record and hit for a .320 average. That was the year of Newark's million dollar infield. Many observers feel that this team was the best in Newark's history, superior even to the World Series winners of 1946.

Leon's biggest thrill in baseball came on opening day of that championship season, when after two-and-a-half years in the Army during World War II, the returning soldier hurled a no-hitter against the Philadelphia Stars in Newark's Ruppert Stadium. No baserunner reached second base and Leon faced only 29 batters. One man reached first on a walk and two by virtue of errors by shortstop Benny Felder, but one of them was erased on a double play. "Felder was just a young kid," Leon remembers. "He could field pretty good, but he wasn't all that sure and he might over-run anything."

One of his errors was controversial. Felder fielded the ball cleanly but took three or four skips before throwing the ball and then made a bad throw. "He should have had him out," Leon says, adding modestly, "but they probably should have given the man a hit." The fans were less objective, heaving a collective sigh of relief when the scoreboard registered an error on the play.

The Stars had some good hitters on their ball club who were frustrated by Leon's pitching prowess, including Bus Clarkson, Gene Benson, and Frank Austin, all of whom were consistent .300 hitters. Austin had led the league in 1944 with a .390 average, and Benson had recorded consecutive averages of .327, .370 and .345 through the 1946 season.

After the end of the season, as a part of Satchel Paige's All-Stars, Benson hit Bob Feller like a cousin while barnstorming against the Hall of Fame great. Day had more success against the left-handed swinger than did his more illustrious major league counterpart, whom Satchel referred to as Bob Rapid. "I pitched in on most left-handers," Leon reveals, "I tried to pitch high and tight or low and inside on them. I kept everything inside, and gave them nothing away. On anything away, Benson used to just slap the ball. He was a pretty good hitter. I threw to him straight over-hand with nothing from the side."

While Leon was near perfect, so was his opponent for the day, Barney Brown. Brown kept the Eagles in check for five innings before Clarence "Pint" Israel bounced a triple off the right-center field wall, and then scored on Larry Doby's clean single to center. That was all that Leon needed to sew up the victory.

But later in the inning the Eagles scored an insurance run on a controversial play that exploded into a brawl and near riot. Doby stole second and tried to score when Philly second-baseman Mahlon Duckett snared a smash off the bat of Lennie Pearson and nipped him at first with a good throw. The relay home appeared to arrive in time for the put-out but Doby was declared safe on a close play at the plate. Catcher Bill Cash, enraged at the call, flailed umpire Pete Strauch with both hands, knocking him to the ground. Playing manager Goose Curry ran in from his right-field position to join the fray and deliver a few swift kicks to the felled umpire. Players from both benches rushed to separate the men. Fans swarmed onto the field and mounted policemen had to be called into action to quell the unruly mob.

Leon watched from the dugout as the brawl spread and turned into a near riot. "When they started fighting I was sitting on the bench and I stayed there," he laughs. But he quickly dismisses the possibility of any adverse affects to his arm due to the interruption of play. "The delay of the game didn't bother me," he says. And the outcome of the game concurs with his assertion. After order was restored, Leon continued his stellar performance.

But, while the delay wasn't long enough for his arm to stiffen, later in the game he suffered an arm injury that limited his effectiveness for the remainder of his career. The play is still vivid in Leon's mind. "Somebody hit a swinging bunt down the third base line and I went over to field it. And when I went to throw, my foot slipped. When I threw it, I could feel something pull. My arm had already been messed up from 1938 and it just started it over again. That was opening day and I never was no good the whole season." The tenacious competitor never said a word to anyone and finished the game despite the pain.

When just one out away from the coveted no-hitter and with pinch-hitter Henry McHenry coming to the plate, one of his Eagle teammates came in to the mound to talk to Leon. "He said, 'Don't throw him anything but fastballs, he's a slow swinger,'" Leon recalls. "That's what they always told me. They said that about everybody." So Leon heeded his teammate's advice and challenged McHenry with his best pitch, a high hard one. "Every pitch I raised it a little," says Leon. "The last one was up around his eyes." Three fastballs later Leon had disposed of McHenry for the final out to earn a 2-0 victory. The triumphant Day was carried off the field by big Johnny Davis and a host of other teammates amidst the Eagle fans' jubilant celebration. Even without the controversial play at home the no-hitter would have remained intact.

Characteristically, Leon is quick to take the spotlight off himself and share it with his opposing moundsman. "I think that Barney only gave up one or two hits," he points out about the fine pitching job turned in by Philadelphia pitcher Barney Brown.

The Eagles went on from there to dethrone the Homestead Grays, ending their nine-year skein of Negro National League pennants, and then defeated the Kansas City Monarchs in the ensuing World Series to reign as the World Champions of black baseball.

◊   ◊   ◊

Despite his near perfect return to the playing field after two-and-a-half years of military service in World War II, Leon was never quite the same player that he had been before the War. Like so many other players, he left a portion of his God-given ability in the rust of prolonged athletic inactivity during his absence from the National Pastime.

Day is carried off the field
by teammates following his opening day no-hitter in 1946.

Japan's surprise attack on Pearl Harbor had caught Leon in Puerto Rico where he was playing winter ball. His team won the second half pennant and Leon won his final five decisions, but neither his team's success nor his 2.93 ERA and .351 batting average seemed of relative importance after such an historic occasion. And with the presence of German submarines in the Atlantic there was some concern about the American players being able to return safely to the United States.

Like most people of his generation, Leon remembers the event vivid-
ly. "When they bombed Pearl Harbor I was down in Ponce, Puerto Rico. I
never will forget it. I wanted to fly back but they wouldn't let us fly, and
they were sinking ships out there in the Atlantic."

In addition to Leon, among the other black American players who
were temporarily stranded in Puerto Rico were Willie Wells, Ray
Dandridge, Josh Gibson, Monte Irvin and Roy Campanella. But Day and
the other Americans were soon able to return to the States in time to open
the baseball season, and after his sensational 1942 performance, Leon extended his mound success on into 1943. In January of the new year, the
Pittsburgh Courier classified him as "the outstanding moundsman in
Negro baseball." Newark's ace hurler lived up to his billing and continued
his winning ways, culminating the season with another appearance in the
all-star game where he allowed only one hit in his two shut-out innings in
an effort to stave off the West's 2-1 victory.

At the season's end, while the Birmingham Black Barons and
Chicago American Giants were having a play-off to determine who would
play the Homestead Grays in the World Series, the Grays stayed in good
playing form by playing a three-game exhibition series against the Negro
National League All-Stars. Needless to say the starting pitcher for the All-
Stars was Leon Day. In what proved to be his last pitching performance
for two years, Leon shut-out the Grays until the sixth inning when they
pushed across a run. The Grays added another in the seventh and Leon's
teammates could muster only one run on his behalf, leaving them on the
short end of a 2-1 score.

By then the country had been thrust fully into the War effort, and this
was to be his last season before Uncle Sam beckoned. A week earlier the
newspapers had headlined, "Newark to lose battery aces." The accompany-
ing story reported how the draft had hit "the team's number one battery,"
and that the two roomies, Day and Ruffin, would be inducted into the
army and navy respectively. Referring to Leon, the article stated, "Day is
one of the greatest pitchers in Newark history."

In September of 1943, while still in his prime, he entered into
military service. Less than a year later, along with three million other soldiers, he was on his way to Normandy. Six days after D-Day he went
ashore at Utah Beach as a member of the 818th Amphibian Battalion.

"When we landed we were pretty close to the action because we
could hear the small arms fire," Leon remembers. "I drove a duck. The
other troops had moved up but we stayed on the beach hauling ammunition and supplies from the ships out in the harbor that were bringing men.
We were under fire. I remember one night when I came out of the water
with a load of ammunition and the Germans started dropping flares and lit

the beach up so bright that you could have read a newspaper. I heard the
planes coming, so I jumped out of the duck and ran up to the bank. A MP
had a hole there, a sandbagged place. I couldn't see him but he said, 'Soldier!' I said, 'Yeah?' He said, 'Come on in here.' So I went in his hole
and I got in there and we were trembling and the planes coming, strafing
everything and shooting everything up on the beach. He said, 'Who's driv-
ing that duck out there?' I said, 'I am.' He said, 'What has it got on it?' I
said, 'Ammunition.' He said, 'Move that duck from out in front of this
hole!' I said, 'Go out there and move it your own damn self!'"

"I was in the combat area about two or three months, until they broke
through and moved out, and we stayed on the beach until after Thanksgiving. By Thanksgiving I think they were on the way to Paris and then we
moved to Le Havre, France. We were in Le Havre when the Germans
broke through in the Battle of the Bulge and that's as far as we got. We
went down into southern France somewhere near Nice at a port down
there, and got some ammunition and brought it back up into France. After
that we stayed right there in Le Havre."

◊   ◊   ◊

Some ballplayers were assigned to special services where they played exhibition games for the duration of the War, thus maintaining their baseball
skills. But Leon didn't touch a baseball until after V-E day when he
pitched against General Patton's Third Army baseball team at Nuremberg,
Germany in what was characterized as the GI World Series.

Never one to be considered a shrinking violet, Patton could be seen
riding around the streets of Nuremberg on a motorcycle, wearing his
holstered pearl-handled pistols. Just as the Third Army had won honors in
combat, his baseball team was expected to win honors on the ballfield.

Harry Walker, who was an outfielder on the St. Louis Cardinals' pennant winners of 1942-43 before entering military service, was one of the
players on the Third Army's team. He gives us an idea of the type of
respect and admiration that General Patton commanded. "The man that
was the most disciplined man in the business, and the guy that everybody
who worked under him were telling him that they were proud to be with
him, and without him we might not have won the war . . . was Patton.
And ever since then we have not had the leadership. We've taken away
from the discipline. Without that firmness, it just breaks down."

Obviously, the baseball team reflected Patton's dedication to excellence. In addition to Walker, the team was comprised of the best talent
available, including major leaguers Ewell Blackwell, Kenny Heintzelman,
Johnny Wyrostek and Benny Zientara. Leon remembers, "They had a
good team up there. They had almost a major league team, with a couple

73

of International League players. They were bragging about how they were going to beat us."

While the Third Army team was loaded with professionals, Leon's OISE (Overseas Invasion Service Expedition) team was composed almost exclusively of semi-pro players. Only Leon, his former Negro World Series adversary Willard Brown, and Russ Bauers from the Pittsburgh Pirates were experienced professionals. The remainder of the squad had only "played on semi-pro teams." Of this aggregation, Day and Brown were the only two black players on the ball club. The team was a heavy underdog and no one expected them to win. "No, I wasn't supposed to beat them," Leon smiles. But that is exactly what he did! He bested the Phillies' Ken Heintzelman and the Third Army's picked professionals by a score of 2-1, while allowing only "four scratch hits."

The major leaguers were wondering where he and Brown had come from. At that point in time Jackie Robinson was a rookie shortstop in his only year in the Negro Leagues, and completely unaware of what Branch Rickey had in mind for him the following winter.

Meanwhile, Leon was in Europe proving to 100,000 GIs that a black man could outplay major leaguers. A decade earlier he had been nervous when playing in front of half that many people at Comiskey Park during his first appearance in the Negro All-Star game. The size of the crowd at the GI World Series really impressed Leon. "I don't know how many soldiers were in there," he says. "They were all over the place." While the number of people present for the game was somewhat awe-inspiring, the major league hitters didn't intimidate him at all. "I was bearing down on them," he explains. The Third Army's most prominent player was Harry Walker, who later won a National League batting title and became an outstanding manager, but who is probably best known for his single in the 1946 World Series that scored Enos Slaughter on his mad dash from first base to the Hall of Fame. Concerning "Harry the Hat," Leon says, "I knew who he was but I never had any trouble with him or any of the major leaguers." After all, as he said, he was bearing down on them.

After Leon had defeated the highly favored Third Army team for the ETO (European Theatre of Operations) Championship, their manager, Captain John Quinn, who in civilian life had been the general manager of the Philadelphia Phillies, wrangled the major leaguers onto the OISE team and they traveled to Italy to play for the MTO (Mediterranean Theatre of Operations) championship against an all-black team who were almost exclusively semi-pro ballplayers.

Leon was opposed to the addition of the major leaguers to their team, and told Quinn, "We should go with the same team that we beat them with. We don't need them. But," Leon continues, "when we got on the plane they were on there. So we went on to Italy, and the boys there didn't have anything." The only player on the team with professional experience was Joe Greene, who had caught for the Kansas City Monarchs, and whom Leon had victimized in the 1942 black all-star game and world series. "He was the only guy that I had seen," Leon says. And although he doesn't remember the exact score of the lopsided contest, he adds, "We run over them easy."

Then in a rematch of the two teams in Nice, France, Day and Brown, who were the only black players on the championship team, were asked to switch sides and play for the black team that they had just beaten. "Quinn walked over and asked me, 'Is it all right if you play with these boys?'", Leon recalls of the changeover. "'Why don't you and Brown go over and play with them, they don't have anything.' I said, 'Yeah, I'll go and play with them.'" So the two Negro League stars switched sides. "It made me mad," the soft spoken competitor admits, and he let his pitching speak for him as he defeated Ewell Blackwell, "eight-to-nobody."

In support of Leon, Willard Brown hit two home runs off the "Whip," as the Cincinnati Reds right-handed sidewinder was nicknamed. "That's the only way we beat him," Leon says, "Brown drove in all the runs." And even though he defeated Blackwell, Leon was favorably impressed with him. "I liked Blackwell," he says. "He had good stuff and he was a nice guy. He wasn't chesty like the rest of them."

"We only played about five games, maybe six," Leon says, summarizing his war-time baseball experience against major league pitchers. "I beat Heintzelman up in Germany and Blackwell down in France. But after that we didn't play any more games."

Those who had futilely tried to hit his sneaky short-arm deliveries in the Negro Leagues before the War would not have been surprised at his mastery of the major leaguers.

◊   ◊   ◊

Leon admits now that his arm never felt the same after the War. "There's one thing about when I was over there. We didn't have any training or nothing. After the war was over, they said we were going to play baseball and we just started right up playing. We hadn't got in any shape and never even got loose. I think that's what messed my arm up when I came back to the states in '46. My arm never did feel right no more."

Leon returned to the States in Feb. of 1946 and six weeks later he was back in an Eagles uniform trying to salvage his interrupted career. But he was never able to completely recapture his previous level of excellence. Although he continued to pitch and compiled a 9-4 worksheet (topping the league in wins, strikeouts, innings pitched and complete games, while contributing a .469 batting average), he never fully recovered from the injury that he suffered in the opening day no-hitter. The injury continued to plague him and he knew his arm would never be the same, yet he persevered and helped his team in the dethronement of the Champion Homestead Grays, ending their nine year domination of the league.

When it came time to select a pitcher to open the World Series against the Kansas City Monarchs at the Polo Grounds, manager Biz Mackey picked Leon Day, sore arm and all, for the task. So in a night game in front of almost 20,000 avid fans, Leon took his overworked right arm to the mound to face the Monarchs' famed curve-master, Hilton Smith. The Monarchs' Hank Thompson, who later went to the majors with the New York Giants, led off the first inning with a single to right field and took third on the fielder's error. Thompson came home on Bonnie Serrell's single with the first run of the game. The Monarchs threatened to score again but Leon tightened down, and retired the side, getting two men on strikeouts, including their star slugger, Willard "Home Run" Brown.

This unearned first-inning run was the only one that he surrendered before leaving the game. When Hilton Smith walked Larry Doby to open the seventh inning, the lanky legend named Satchel Paige who was constantly crossing Leon's career path, ambled out to the mound to save the day for the Monarchs. But before the tall right-hander could put out the fire, Doby had stolen second base and scored on Johnny Davis' base hit to tie the game at 1-1. The score remained unchanged when Leon made his exit, thus neither starting pitcher was on the scene at the end of the game. Satchel remained on the mound to get credit for the victory when his team rallied against Rufus Lewis, who finished for the Eagles and took the loss.

With their backs to the wall where another loss would mean a victory for the Monarchs in the Series, the Eagles again turned to Leon in their hour of need. A team man all the way, he responded to his team's need and dragged his aching arm to the mound one time too many.

He just didn't have anything left in his arm and he knew it, but he made a valiant effort. After hitting Chico Renfroe to open the game, and suffering from two Eagle errors, he was rocked by Willard Brown's home run in the first inning. Unable to continue on the mound, he finished the game in the outfield, where the fleet-footed Day showed that he was an all-around player. The newspapers applauded Leon's display of his versatility when he made a "sensational over the shoulder catch" of Buck O'Neil's smash to left-center field.

While scouts from the Brooklyn Dodgers and New York Giants watched from the stands, Leon's teammate, Monte Irvin, smashed two

The 1946 Negro League Champion Newark Eagles. Leon Day is seated on the extreme right. Other players include their keystone combination, shortstop Monte Irvin and second baseman Larry Doby, standing on the extreme left and right, respectively.

home runs to highlight the Eagles' offensive barrage that overcame the early Kansas City lead, knotting the series at three games apiece.

Newark also won the rubber seventh game to reign as champions of black baseball. Shortly afterwards Leon celebrated his 30th birthday and although chronologically still in the prime of his life, he was already a veteran of one war and thirteen years in professional baseball. As a member of the World Champions of Black Baseball, he had reached the pinnacle of success. This lofty perch was something that he could never have foreseen as a youngster with an unquenchable thirst for baseball.

◊   ◊   ◊

Leon Day was born October 30, 1916 in Alexandria, Virginia but his family moved to Mount Winans, Maryland when he was only six months old. It was there that the youngster grew up loving and playing baseball. His home was not too far from Westport Park where the Baltimore Black Sox played. The Black Sox were one of the best black ball clubs in the country, and young Leon would go over to the ballpark every Sunday and watch them play. "It was within walking distance but it was a good walk, about two miles. I'd go over the fence, under the fence, or sometimes I'd get a foul ball and they'd let me in. Just any way I could get in, I'd get in there."

The Sox boasted an aggregation of talented baseball players, including Boogum Wilson, Dick Lundy, Oliver Marcelle, Frank Warfield, Martin Dihigo, Rap Dixon, Pete Washington, and Scrip Lee. Their infield of Marcelle at third base, Lundy at shortstop, Warfield at second base, and Wilson at first base was the greatest in the history of the Negro leagues until the Newark Eagles' million dollar infield of Leon's time.

The youngster appreciated the superlative play of these early greats, but his personal favorite was their pitching ace, Laymon Yokely. "He was a good pitcher," Leon recalls. "He threw hard and he could strike guys out. He had one pitch that I ain't never seen anybody hit. He'd wind up and throw his hand behind his back before he threw the ball." Leon chuckles when here counts how one die-hard fan encouraged the motion that Yokely made when he threw the pitch. "There was an old guy who used to walk the fence and one day he was in the stands. He'd say, 'Come on Yokely! Come on Yokely!' and you could hear his voice all over the ballpark. And when Yokely would get two strikes on the batter, he would yell louder than ever," imploring the Black Sox hurler to strike out the batter. Invariably, Yokely would accommodate the request, resorting to his unique motion for the third strike.

Leon played ball out in the field with other kids his age, using a broomstick and tennis ball until around the age of twelve, when he began playing sandlot baseball with the Mount Winans Athletic Club. After a few years with them, he left and caught on as a second baseman with a semi-pro team called the Silver Moons. It was mostly "semi" and very little "pro." They promised him two dollars a game but sometimes he got the two dollars and sometimes he got the promise. While with the Silver Moons, perhaps foretelling his future path to greatness, whenever a pitcher got into a jam, the confident second sacker would say, "Give *me* the ball." And when the ball was handed to him, he would get the job done.

The talented youngster stayed with the Silver Moons less than a full season. "That's when Rap came through," he explains. Mac Eggleston, the catcher and manager of the Silver Moons, had once played for the Black Sox and, impressed with what he saw from the budding star, sent Leon to see Rap Dixon, the playing manager of the Black Sox. Rap told the hard-throwing youngster to be ready to leave the following weekend. The eager Leon had to get his father's permission first. The elder Day asked his anxious son, "Is that what you really want to do?" "That's the only thing I want to do" was the honest response. "Well if that's what you want, go ahead" his father replied. Thus, in the spring of 1934 the aspiring athlete went to spring training with the team that he had admired as a boy. The team had deserted Baltimore and were now playing out of Chester, Pennsylvania. Most of his boyhood favorites had also departed and the Black Sox at this time possessed a dearth of athletic talent.

However, some of the old-time players were still around. One of them was the man who signed him, Rap Dixon. "He was still playing," Leon reflects. "He wasn't in his prime but he could still hit the ball."

Another great hitter from the old-time Black Sox was Jud "Boogum" Wilson, who was with the league champion Philadelphia Stars. During a game against the Stars at Chester, Rap Dixon ordered his young pitcher to throw at his former Black Sox teammate. In retrospect, Leon laughs when recounting the incident, but at the time it was no laughing matter. "Rap made me throw at Boogum. He said, 'Hey youngster, you see that son-of-a-bitch right there.' I said, 'Yes sir.' He said, 'When he comes to bat the next time, throw at him. I mean throw at him! You hear?' I said, 'Yes sir, Mr. Dixon.' So I threw at old Boogum and I threw hard too. And I hit him! Old Boogum looked at me and said, 'You son-of-a-bitch, if you hit me again, goddamn it, I'm going to kill you. You hear me?' I said 'Yes sir, Mr. Boogum.' I didn't hit him no more either!"

Leon remembered Boogum from the days when he had watched the Black Sox as a youngster in Baltimore. Boogum was one of the roughest players in the league and nobody messed with him. Or as Leon says, "Nobody *living!*" Then he adds, "Not even the police. Boogum used to fight them in Baltimore. It would take the whole police department to lock him up. He'd knock them down just as fast as they'd get up, and they'd hit him in the head with that billy and he wasn't feeling nothing. Boogum was crazy. He was crazy! I ain't kidding. But Rap made me throw at him. He was the manager, so I just threw at him."

For performing services such as this brush with potential disaster, Dixon had promised him $60 a month which looked like a fortune to the 17-year-old. But he didn't even get that much. The team was playing on a percentage basis and when they divided up the day's take, they would give Leon a couple of dollars and he never knew what the others were getting. "They were playing on a percentage but I didn't know it then," he remembers. "After the end of a game, I noticed all the older players would go on in the room and they would leave me outside. Rap would come out there and give me two or three dollars. They were cutting it up five or eight dollars a man. And he would give me a dollar or two dollars and I would go on and get me some ice cream and a comic book and I was ready. I would eat that ice cream and get in bed and read those comic books. And never got no money!"

The Black Sox were added to the Negro National League for the second half of the season but had a dismal record. Along about this time Buck Leonard, star first baseman of the Homestead Grays, saw Leon pitch and was sufficiently impressed to make him an offer of $125 a month to play with the Grays. Buck, now a member of the Baseball Hall of Fame, remembers when he first saw Day. "He had a good fastball and a good curve, and I asked him if he wanted to play with the Grays. He turned out to be one of the best pitchers in our league."

Leon jumped at the chance to go with the Grays since he was actually getting only about half of the $60 a month that he was promised. "Buck tried to steal me," he recalls of the circumstances that almost led to him becoming a member of the Homestead club. "We played in Johnstown, Pennsylvania one night and I struck out about 15. I blinded them. Then we went to Pittsburgh and he was trying to get me to go to the Grays. Buck talked to me in front of the hotel where we were staying and he asked me how much I was making. I told him $60 a month and he said, 'Come on over here with us and we'll give you a hundred and a quarter.' I said, 'That sounds pretty good,' and I was going, too. I went on upstairs and got my little cardboard suitcase that I had and packed my stuff and was easing on down the steps. And old Rap Dixon caught me. He said, 'Hey boy, where you going?' I said, 'I'm going on over there with the Grays.' He said, 'You ain't going nowhere. Take that bag on back up the steps. Your father told me when you left home to bring you back. And that's what you're going to do.'" And that's what Leon did! He turned right around and took his suitcase back upstairs and forgot about going to the Grays. But according to Leon, Rap was not exactly true to his word.

"He may have told my daddy that he'd get me home but he left me stranded in Chester, Pennsylvania when the season was over. I woke up one morning and everybody was gone but me! Nobody was in town but me and Sonny Harris. He said, 'Where is everybody?' I said, 'I don't know.'" The two abandoned ballplayers went on down to a Greek Restaurant where the team ate on the tab and ordered their usual breakfast, but the owner said, "Not today. Jack Farrell, he no pay. You no eat."

So two hungry and angry players went looking for Jack Farrell, the owner of the team. They found him downtown shooting dice at the local pool hall which doubled as a gambling joint. Harris, who was "a big tall dude," said "give me my damn money home!" And little Leon quickly interjected, "Me too!" In deference to their mood, the high rolling Farrell endeavored to placate the two disgruntled players and gave them their traveling money. Leon's share was $2, which was all it cost to get a bus ticket home from there.

"But I was going with the Grays and turn pro if it hadn't been for Rap," Leon reminds us. His old skipper may have thwarted Leon's first opportunity at the black big time but, even though Rap had left him stranded the previous season, he didn't forget about his protege. Dixon left the Black Sox and went to the Brooklyn Eagles in 1935, and took Leon with him.

"Rap got in touch with me," Leon says, recounting the day he left home. "He came by my house and asked me if I wanted to go." At his tender age Leon couldn't go without his father's permission. The elder Day knew that his son wanted desperately to be a ballplayer and, although his father had some misgivings, he didn't try to dissuade Leon. But he did offer some parting advice. "My daddy gave me a little penknife and told me to put it in my pocket. He said, 'You meet a lot of people when you travel.'" His father's admonition was well deserved for in the business of black baseball there were some rowdy individuals, and a youngster on the road had to be cautious of the company that he kept.

Having received his father's approval, Leon embarked on his first major venture away from home. "The bus came down and picked me up at Mt. Winans and we went down to spring training together," remembers Leon. The Eagles were training in Jacksonville, Florida and the teenager was more than a little bit homesick. Besides fighting the homesick blues, he had something else to be concerned with. There were some outstanding players on hand in camp including George Giles, Harry Williams, Tex Burnette, Ed Stone, Double Duty Radcliffe, Fats Jenkins and Bill Yancey. The latter two players were standouts in both baseball and basketball, having played basketball professionally with the Knickerbockers. The competition was pretty stiff for a rookie trying to break into black baseball's big time.

One day Candy Jim Taylor, the Eagles' manager, told Leon to throw batting practice. The raw youngster pitched without a windup and short-armed the ball, cocking the ball right behind his ear to throw and coming three-quarters overhand. He had developed this unorthodox style from playing second base and had just carried it to the mound. Nobody showed him how to pitch. "That's the only way I could throw," Leon says. But despite his unusual delivery, he had pinpoint control and a blazing fastball that the batters couldn't hit.

Watching Leon's performance closely, the wiley veteran skipper promptly turned him into a regular pitcher, and the 5'10", 178-pound right-hander responded by becoming the ace of the staff. In addition to his fastball Leon had a good curve and a change of pace, and as he says, "That was about it." And that was all that he needed. The rookie pitched the opening day of the season and continued his impressive twirling throughout the year. In early May he spun a stylish five-hitter to defeat Webster McDonald and the defending champion Philadelphia Stars, and went on from there to fashion a successful record against the best bats in black baseball.

Veteran pitcher-catcher Ted "Double-Duty" Radcliffe helped the young pitcher by teaching him a pick-off move to first base, which Leon perfected. Although this half-balk move is now illegal, at that time it was not only legal but also very effective. Leon regularly caught baserunners off guard with the ploy, much to the pleasure of his manager.

Taylor was not the only one to appreciate the young fireballer's talent. He was selected to play in the annual East-West classic, the Negro league all-star game, at Comiskey Park in Chicago. The West lineup included Hall-of Famers Josh Gibson, Oscar Charleston, Buck Leonard, and Cool Papa Bell as well as potential Hall-of-Famers Willie Wells and Mule Suttles. Facing such formidable opposition, the youngster was appropriately apprehensive in his first all-star appearance. Or as Leon succinctly phrases it, "I was scared to death! There were over 50,000 people in that park. I was nervous because I hadn't ever seen that many people. I was just like I was in a daze or in a trance."

Slim Jones, the Lefty Grove of the Negro Leagues, had started the game and "he was loose. He was really throwing that ball hard." After the tall southpaw finished his three scoreless innings, the 19-year-old Day took the mound at the beginning of the fourth frame to protect a 2-0 lead. As fate would have it, the first batter that he faced was the legendary slugger, Josh Gibson, who greeted Leon with a sizzling double to center field.

The youngster was still a bit unsettled but he quickly quieted his but-
terflies and retired the side without giving up a run.

Leon was in complete control in the fifth, setting the side down in
order, two on called third strikes. But in the sixth frame, the West made a
move to blow the game open with a big inning by sending up sluggers
Turkey Stearnes and Buck Leonard to pinch-hit. Day quickly disposed of
Stearnes, another Hall of Fame candidate, who skied to center field on
Leon's first delivery. Then Buck Leonard advanced to the plate, also
making his first appearance in an all-star game.

Left-hander Luis Tiant, Sr., father of the well-known Luis Tiant who
later starred in the American League in the 1960's, was warming up in
the bullpen. Buck, a left-hander, was noted as a fastball hitter who was
especially tough on right-handers. The logical decision would have been
to play the percentages and bring in the veteran Tiant. But the young
rookie was allowed to stay in the game and Leon justified their confidence by forcing Buck to ground weakly back to the box to end the inning.

In the seventh inning, Gibson knocked in Bell with a wind-blown
double that could have been caught. Mule Suttles, who could hit them just
as far as Josh, strode to the plate. In the stands the fans were yelling,
"Mule! Kick donkey!", encouraging Suttles to repeat his heroics of two
years earlier when his home run had won the inaugural contest. But Leon
had other ideas. He bore down on the Mule and struck him out, ending
the threat.

Leon left the game with the score tied and, despite poor fielding support, he had pitched well in his four inning stint, striking out three while
walking only two batters. Certainly not a bad performance for a rookie.

Little did anyone suspect that four innings later Suttles would win the
game for the West with an encore round-tripper off Martin Dihigo in the
eleventh inning. "Dihigo came in from center field to pitch to him and he
hit that ball a country mile!," Leon exclaims, with the Mule's game-winning blast still clear in his mind.

The all-star game appearance was indicative of the type of season
that the freshman hurler encountered. While his team was not very successful, he personally had a good year. His performance was rewarded
when, after the season, the Eagles picked up a few additional players and
went to Puerto Rico for the winter season. It was to be the first of several
winters that he spent in the land "where the sunlight dances off the
ocean." But back home in Newark, another new experience awaited the
nineteen-year-old. A great team was in the making.

The Brooklyn Eagles had been a losing ball club in 1935, but after
the season Abe Manley bought the Newark Dodgers' franchise and com-

bined the two teams. "The Dodgers had some pretty good ballplayers but I guess they didn't have room for all of them," Leon reflects. Fortunately for the Eagles, one of the two players who came from the Dodgers was hot-corner magician Ray Dandridge. Thus, in 1936 Manley's team became the Newark Eagles, and the ingredients were present to produce a winning team.

In a 1935 game between the two clubs before they consolidated, only 300 patrons had come out to see them play, while in the same area 2500 fans saw the Philadelphia Stars play an East Orange semi-pro team.

But things began to change in '36. The Eagles finished strong that year, claiming second place behind the great Pittsburgh Crawfords for the second half of the split season. The other baseball team in town, the Newark Bears, were the New York Yankees' top farm team and under the direction of Vice President George Weiss, had attained a reputation of being virtually a major league caliber ball club. Their roster was annually filled with the players who were to nurture the Yankee dynasty for years to come. After the close of league play the Eagles tried to get an exhibition series against the Bears, but the International League commissioner would not sanction the Bears' participation.

◊   ◊   ◊

The following year the Eagles had completely assembled their famous million-dollar infield of Ray Dandridge at third base, Willie Wells at shortstop, Dick Seay at second base, and Mule Suttles at first base. They were given their nickname based on their worth had they been white. Complementing the infield finesse was a two-pronged pitching staff comprised of Leon Day and Terris McDuffie, which gave them the mound strength they needed to make a serious run for the pennant. The duo carried the bulk of the workload, much like the 1948 Boston Braves' combination of Spahn and Sain of a decade later.

Both on and off the field, the two Eagle hurlers were opposites. McDuffie was provocative and self-centered, always demanding and expecting the spotlight. By contrast, Leon was a quiet, proficient team player, and quick to give credit to others. McDuffie got the most ink, but Leon got the most wins.

In a tough tussle with the Homestead Grays, who were just beginning to establish their dynasty, the Eagles finished second again. Leon had one of his best seasons and when not pitching, played in the outfield or at second base much of the time because he was also a good right-handed hitter. Selected again to the all-star squad, he not only pitched shut-out ball but doubled in his only plate appearance to help the East defeat the West by a score of 7-2.

Day (right) with Manager Biz Mackey and owner Effa Manley
prior to a 1946 Negro World Series game.
(Photo courtesy of Larry Hogan.)

The all-star game almost didn't come off because of a mini-strike by
the East squad for more money. "When I went out there in '35 I didn't
get anything but hotel room and meals," Leon says. "They would just pay
our way out and weren't paying us anything, noway." Since then the
owners had raised the ante to where "they were paying us $25 or $30."
But the players wanted a larger slice of the pie. "Josh was the leader,"
Leon continues. "We all got together in the clubhouse before the game
and said we wanted more money. Chester Williams was there and spoke

up. Everybody had a little say. All the owners were there. Mrs. Manley came down to talk to us players that she had on the team. She asked me, 'Are you going on strike?' I said, 'Yeah, I'm going on strike. Everybody else is going on strike and I'm going too.' She said, 'I didn't think you would do anything like that.' After we got our money everything was all right." Leon's performance in the game surely showed that, for the East at least, everything was truly all right.

◊   ◊   ◊

After two winters in Puerto Rico, Leon made his first trip to Cuba at the end of the season. Leon regards the Cubans as "better native ballplayers than any place else even though the country is only a small island." As a special attraction a game was arranged between the Cuban All-Stars and the American All-Stars. In addition to Day, the American squad featured Josh Gibson, Ray Dandridge, Willie Wells, Raymond Brown, and Sam Bankhead.

But in a repeat of the East-West game preliminary showdown, the American players went on strike for more money. They were offered $25 but held out for $50. Josh Gibson acted as their spokesman and the players stayed in the clubhouse until they got their money. The atmosphere in the locker room was somewhat different than it had been in Chicago, when Mrs. Manley remonstrated with the players. Dolph Luque, a former pitcher with the Cincinnati Reds, was in charge of the players. "We stayed in the clubhouse," Leon remembers, describing the situation. "Luque was madder than the devil. He said, 'Goddamn it, if you guys want to go on home, go on home!' He was walking around with his pistol. He tried to scare us out on the field. The ballpark was packed. We said, 'We ain't going out until we get the money,' and he finally got it up. He paid us just before game time."

After they started taking in American players, the Cuban league was the toughest in Latin America. Playing against this level of competition, Leon proved to be Almendares' leading pitcher and logged a 7-3 record for the short winter season. But with a bright future ahead, catastrophe struck in a most unlikely way. While showering after a game, Leon slipped in the shower room and injured his throwing arm. "I had on those old wooden shower shoes and when I slipped, I was falling back and I reached back to catch myself. And when I did, I heard something pop back in my shoulder."

Leon went on to Florida for spring training with the Eagles and tried to pitch, but his arm hurt so bad that he couldn't continue and he missed the entire season. "I just couldn't do it, I couldn't throw," he says, remem-

bering the pain. "I didn't play in 1938. My arm was bad." The Eagles did
not fare well without his services on the mound and subsequently dropped
out of contention for the pennant, finishing the second half just one step
out of the cellar.

This was prior to the Nautilus era and before the days of modern
medical diagnosis and techniques. "They took me down to Trenton and
the trainer worked on me," Leon says. But they couldn't prescribe anything to correct the condition, so Leon took it upon himself to be his own
physical therapist. All during the off-season he worked out with two irons,
loosening and strengthening his arm. The next spring he was determined
to get his arm well and he literally "threw the soreness out of it."

Leon recalls his initial misgivings about coming back. "In 1939 we
went to Daytona Beach and I got my legs in shape, but I was kind of
scared to throw. I tossed and never felt nothing and then I started to throw
hard, really cutting loose. And I never had any more trouble until I got
out of the army eight years later."

Manager Dick Lundy was instrumental in helping to bring Leon's
arm around gradually. At times Leon was anxious to find out if he had his
old stuff, but Lundy was patient and never let him push himself too soon.
Behind the plate, Leon had another source of assistance to help him in his
comeback effort. Day's roomie, Leon Ruffin, and Johnny Hayes, both outstanding receivers were good at handling pitchers and offered encourage-
ment to the recuperating ace. Ruffin "carried a weak stick," but there was
no one to whom Day preferred to pitch.

Leon gave his arm the first serious test in Macon, Georgia on the first
Sunday in May, when he pitched a full nine innings to defeat the Atlanta
Black Crackers, defending champions of the Negro American league. The
newsmen wrote that "his arm seemed to have completely regained it's
former strength," and that "everyone was highly elated." The Eagles arrived from spring training "cocky and confident" and, with Leon returning
to form, were back in contention, challenging the Grays again for the pennant. The rejuvenated ace opened on the mound for Lundy's charges, but
had some control problems. Lundy reassured his star that, not only would
he pitch again, he would win his next start. True to Lundy's prediction, in
the next outing, Leon tossed a six-hit shutout and knocked in the only run
of the game with a double. By mid-August the *Newark Herald* wrote that
Day was "running up an enviable string of victories," but the Eagles were
still falling short in their efforts to dislodge the Grays from atop the
league.

Having regained his previous playing form, Leon was again selected
to play in the all-star game. In the mid-season classic he pitched three hit-
less innings and left the game with his team retaining a 2-0 lead, which

they later squandered in the last two innings. At the end of the season, the
Eagles played in a four-team play-off but were eliminated by the Baltimore Elite Giants.

Following the disappointment of the post-season elimination, Leon
went back to Puerto Rico for another winter. This time he went, not as
part of a barnstorming all-star team, but to play in the first season of their
professional baseball league. At 7:00 AM sharp on a cold October morning, Leon opened the season on the mound for Aquadilla at Eagle's
Ballpark. Leon made the league's debut unforgettable by striking out the
first three batters to face him. After the memorable beginning he pitched
superbly, maintaining his marvelous form throughout the nine innings to
post a 6-0 shutout over Santurce.

A few months later, on January 7, 1940, another cold and windy Sunday morning, these same two clubs met again and one of the all-time
great pitching duels resulted. None present could have possibly had any
idea that they were about to see a piece of baseball history in the making.
Leon was on the mound again for Aquadilla, and pitching for Santurce
was spitball ace Bill Byrd from the Baltimore Elite Giants. Aquadilla
scored a run in the first inning and Santurce matched it in the fourth
frame. From then on it was nothing but a classic pitcher's battle, as Day
and Byrd matched goose-eggs until the eighteenth inning when the game
was suspended because of darkness. Characteristically, Leon is quick to
praise his adversary of the day. "Bill Byrd was a tough pitcher," he says.
"You had to get in front of him early. The longer that the game goes, the
tougher he gets. He used to throw a spitball. You had to get to him early
if you were going to beat him. He was good." Although Byrd matched
Day's run allotment, he couldn't keep up with his strikeouts, as Leon established a new record with a total of nineteen.

In addition to his sensational pitching, when not on the mound Leon
played in the outfield and recorded a respectable .330 batting average.
From Puerto Rico he flew down to Caracas, Venezuela where he teamed
up with his Eagle teammate, Ray Dandridge. "We broke up the league
down there," Leon says. "I had won 12 and lost 1. That's why the league
broke up, because we were winning so much. Our team, Vargas, was running away with the league."

In an effort to retain a semblance of league competitiveness,
Maracaibo signed Josh Gibson and Bill Byrd. Once again, Day and Byrd
matched arms in a classic showdown. "In those foreign countries, we
would always hook up together," Leon explains. "We were the stars." In
early April, in a shortened replay of the Puerto Rican marathon duel two
months earlier, Leon again bested the black spitball ace. Josh Gibson

The 1939-40 Aquadilla baseball team.
Pitching star Leon Day (kneeling second from left) established
a new Puerto Rican league record for strike-outs in a single game with 19.
(Photo courtesy of Luis Alvelo.)

doubled and scored the only run against Leon, who scattered five hits while registering eleven strikeouts. Ray Dandridge stopped the game from the darkness that ended the previous encounter with a game-winning home run in the bottom of the eleventh inning.

When the league broke up, Ray and Leon returned home before the season was over in the States. But they didn't stay long enough to get back into an Eagle uniform. They had been making about $175 a month with Newark and when they were offered $350 a month to go to Mexico, they jumped like Mexican jumping beans. The two took a plane to Mexico where they were joined on the Vera Cruz team by Eagle team-mate Willie Wells and the Grays' great Josh Gibson. Then, like the four horsemen of the apocalypse they ravaged the Mexican League, walking away with the title "by about 15 games," and not looking back.

◊   ◊   ◊

Off the field, Leon had a memorable experience in Mexico that left more than a little impression on him. The team traveled by train over some mountainous terrain, and on this particular occasion they had a train wreck. "We were coming out of Guadalajara on the way to Mexico City and the train ran off the track," Leon says, recreating the scenario. "We had just got out of Guadalajara and hadn't got up no speed. It's a good thing that it wasn't going very fast up in the mountains there. It scared me. I didn't even know it at first. I felt a little bump and Theolic Smith said, 'This train ran off the track.' I didn't believe him. And sure enough, the train stopped and we went out and looked. The train had run off the track and the coach was leaning over like it was going to fall over, so I jumped out and got on the ground." Leon laughs now when recalling the incident, but at the time it was no laughing matter. "It took quite a while for them to get the train back on the track. We stayed there in Guadalajara until they got it straightened up. I didn't sleep at all that night. I wanted to find another way to go to Mexico City but . . .", Leon trails off and laughs again remembering his reaction to the experience.

When they went down to Mexico the Negro National League banned the players from league play for five years, but rescinded the ban after only one year. That's when Leon came back. At the end of the Mexican League season he returned to the States and rejoined Newark. The league officials issued a position statement that the players, as a condition to their reinstatement, were being fined $100. The news release was merely a face-saving gesture for the public's benefit since the players never paid the fine and the league never tried to force the issue.

With their star pitcher back in the fold the Eagles continued to challenge the Grays for the league title but were still unable to dethrone them. "They had Josh and Buck over there hitting that ball over the fence," asserts Leon. The Grays had some other good ballplayers who "set the table" for the Grays' great power tandem. "I pitched harder against them than I did Josh and Buck," he continues, reasoning, "You had to keep them off the bases." That way when the black versions of Babe Ruth and Lou Gehrig did hit the long ball, there was less damage done.

Leon usually was successful against the Grays' batters, including the two sluggers whom the press dubbed "the thunder twins." Leon is credited with being the only player to ever strike out Hall of Fame slugger Buck Leonard three times in one game. Although Buck denies that

Dandy and Day ready to board the plane for Mexico in 1940.
(Photo courtesy of Ray Dandridge.)

anybody ever accomplished this feat against him, he does remember the heated competition between the two teams, and recalls that in his 23 years of professional baseball, the only time that he ever sacrificed a man to second base was against Leon Day.

The historic occurrence came with the two teams playing in Newark in front of a record-breaking crowd. Leon was cruising along with a 2-0 lead over the Grays, when in the last inning they got the tying runs on base. With Josh Gibson following Buck in the batting order, manager Vic Harris instructed Buck to "take one swing and then bunt." Buck fouled his allotted swing down the right field line and then, following orders, sacrificed the tying runs into scoring position. Leon then fired two fastballs by Gibson, the home run king of the Negro Leagues. Then after missing with a third fastball, Day tried a curve. Josh, a notorious curve ball hitter, found the delivery a little bit too much to his liking, and the Hall of Fame superstar smashed it over the scoreboard in center field for a game-winning home run.

The competition between the two contending teams was intense. Baserunnners jumping at infielders, pitchers knocking down batters, and fights resulting from such incidents were commonplace when the two teams squared off on the diamond. Aggressive shortstop Willie Wells was the most frequent target for the Grays' pitchers. "They threw at him like he was a rat," says Leon. Wells was forced to wear a modified coal-miner's helmet to the plate in self defense against the pitchers' retaliatory tactics. Needless to say, the first pitch was right at his head, but the battler got back up and hit the next pitch for a triple.

Sometimes the tension extended to the stands and the fans became in-volved. "We were playing the Grays," Leon recalls of one such incident, "and Chester Williams threw a bat up in the stands. People started throw-ing bottles out there and the cops had to come out there. They were trying to get to Chester." The Eagles-Grays rivalry was not the only one that sometimes resulted in beanball battles. The players carried their style of play with them into the Caribbean when they traveled there to play winter ball.

That winter Leon returned to Puerto Rico and led the league with 168 strikeouts, posted a 2.93 ERA, and hit .351 while playing with Aquadilla. When the competition there became fierce, beanballs were common. During these times pitchers were obligated to protect their teammates by retaliating in kind.

Leon recalls one beanball battle between Chet Brewer and himself. "Me and old Chet Brewer got in a knockdown duel. Chet Brewer threw hard, and he was knocking my men down . . . boom! boom! boom! I said, 'That's alright,' and I went out there and started knocking them suckers down . . . boom! boom! boom! I'd knock them down. So the next inning, he'd knock us down. And I'd knock them down. So I came to bat and I said, 'I know Chet ain't going to throw at me because I'm pitching.' You know, that sucker almost hit me in the *head!* I just did get out of the way!" "You had to have guts if you were going to play", his Newark buddy Ray Dandridge says of their style of play.

"We would always do that," Leon continues. "If I'd be pitching and the other team's pitcher threw at one of my players, then I'd throw at one of his players. We got so one time I would throw at the pitcher. He'd knock one of my men down and I'd go out there and he'd come up to bat and I'd knock him down."

Nobody was excluded from being dusted off. Leon's old nemesis from the Grays and former teammate in Mexico, Josh Gibson, was having a super season, winning the triple crown and the MVP Award. One day Josh engaged Leon in a conversation that led to talk about the practice of pitchers knocking down batters. Leon delves into his reservoir of memories to reconstruct the conversation. "Old Josh told me one time, 'You can't hit me.' I said, 'Yes I *can,* too'. Josh said, 'No you can't.' I was messing around. I was playing with Aquadilla and he was with Santurce. He came to bat and I threw him a slow curveball outside and he leaned over and he looked at it. You know how he used to hit. He raised up and got back. Then I threw one about a foot behind him and he backed into it. It hit him . . . boom! Just like a base drum! And he looked at me and he had the bat in his hand, and he started out there and I said, 'Well, you've got to catch me.' I thought he was coming out on the mound. But he finally threw the bat down and went on to first base. I hit him dead in the ribs. He thought I was going to hit him in the head. I knew I could hit him!"

Josh Gibson was the premier slugger of the Negro Leagues. Regardless of the country, he was foremost among the league's batters. "He hit everywhere," Leon says in confirmation, and is quick to point out, "He was fast, too, for a big man. That sucker could run for a big man. He could move!" Leon adds, "He was a pretty good receiver, and I liked pitching to him. He was a little weak on pop flies. Sometimes, if I was pitching and he was catching, and a pop fly went up right over his head, I would come and get it."

Josh was still in his prime then but "he was drinking," and he had begun to manifest some of the behavior patterns that later became more pronounced as he started his downhill slide. Leon was living in the same apartment as Josh when he almost dropped his wife out of a second story window. The big catcher was holding her by the ankles and dangling her out of the window before people could get to him and calm him down.

"He just went off," Leon explains. Nobody seemed to know what triggered his erratic behavior. It has variously been attributed to excessive drinking, drugs, a mental condition, or some combination of these factors.

In any event the deterioration continued for the next few years and when Leon returned from his military service, the change was readily apparent. He remembers sadly, "I came out of the Army in '46 and he was playing with the Grays and they had Josh catching and he couldn't even bend down. He kinda caught half standing up. It was a shame. I said, 'It's a damn shame for the owner to have a man, the greatest they've got, catching like that.'"

While Josh was beginning to show signs that would eventually lead to his demise as a great player, a new star was just developing in the Puerto Rican League. Originally scheduled to be the man to be the first black to play in the major leagues, Monte Irvin was hitting his stride as a player. Analyzing his former teammate, Leon reflects, "I think Monte developed in Puerto Rico. I played with him at Newark. We played on the same team. He wasn't that good of a hitter when he first started at Newark. He was a good outfielder and played infield pretty good. He had a good strong arm but he might throw the ball over the grandstand and all that kind of junk. But he was just a youngster then. One year he went down there in Puerto Rico and when I saw him down there he was hitting that ball and he was throwing more accurate. That's when he started playing good ball."

On returning to the States, Monte joined a Newark aggregation that he characterizes as more talented than the championship team of 1946. The Eagles that year might have beaten the Grays if the Manleys had been able to hold the team together. Irvin's departure to Mexico, soon followed by Ray Dandridge's return South of the Border, and the trading away of Bus Clarkson served to decimate the squad. Only Leon's brilliant pitching kept the team in the scramble for the flag.

◊   ◊   ◊

Half a decade and a world war later, in 1947, when Dandridge, who was managing in Mexico, came back north to sign players for millionaire owner Jorge Pasquel, he looked up Day and his catcher Leon Ruffin. But this was after the War and Day's arm wasn't the same anymore. "I said, 'Danny I can't go down there, my arm is bad.' He said, 'Come on down and make some of this money.'" Those were the magic words . . . they left the next day. But first the two Leons, Day and Ruffin, went to see Mrs. Manley to give her a chance to match the money so they could stay with Newark. "I went to see Mrs. Manley and told her what offer they had made and she said, 'I can't pay that kind of money.' I said, 'Well,

Mrs. Manley, I'll see you.'" Ruffin echoed, "Me too," and followed Day to Mexico.

This was during the time when Pasquel was raiding the major leagues for players and Leon played against Max Lanier, Sal Maglie, Mickey Owen, and the other major league jumpers for the next two years. He still had a bad arm and in the higher altitude his curve didn't break, his fastball lost it's hop, and more importantly he lost his control. "I couldn't hardly throw a strike," he says, "It looked like the plate moved on me. I could always throw a strike before, so I knew it was my arm. It had to be my arm."

After the 1948 summer season in Mexico, Leon stopped off in Cuba for their winter season before returning to the States. But the league broke up down there and when Leon returned home the Manleys had sold the team and the new owner decided to move the ball club to Houston, Texas.

"That was about the end of it," Leon recalls. "I was with them. They said they were going to send me to Texas and I said I wasn't going to Texas. That was too far away from home. I didn't like the way the man talked, saying I had to go. I told them I wasn't going and they traded me to the Elites."

The Baltimore Elite Giants won the pennant that year, but the league was a severely weakened one. While Leon was in Mexico, Jackie Robinson had broken the unwritten color barrier which prohibited black athletes from playing in the major leagues. Now the other club owners were following suit and signing their own black players. Consequently the Negro Leagues began losing players and the quality of the competition decreased drastically.

The Elites also wanted to develop several young arms, including Joe Black, who later starred as the Brooklyn Dodgers' relief ace in 1952. Consequently Leon's playing time was curtailed considerably.

After another winter in Puerto Rico, the veteran pitcher started another season with the Elites, but was not satisfied with his situation in Baltimore. When offered the chance to sign with Winnipeg in the Canadian League, Leon took advantage of the opportunity. Around mid-season of the following year, eighteen seasons after his first appearance as a professional baseball player and still hanging a sore arm in his sleeve, Leon moved to the highest level of organized baseball short of the major leagues, playing with Toronto in the AAA International League. While being used sparingly, and mostly in relief, Leon "did pretty good." Leon explains, "I went up about half way through the season and I didn't get to play much because they were trying to develop those young boys."

The next year, in 1952, he played with Scranton in the AA Eastern League where he compiled a 13-9 record on the mound and batted a cool

.314. "I did pretty good there," is Leon's modest appraisal of his performance.

At the end of the season he barnstormed with Roy Campanella's all-stars, along with Willie Mays, Monte Irvin and Hank Thompson. "The way that it was, Campy had most of the colored major leaguers, and then he picked guys like myself who had never been in the major leagues. And we played against Whitey Ford, Gil Hodges, and Don Newcombe and those guys. They had an all-major league team. I think the most I ever made on tour was $600 for one game. But some of the guys made five or six times as much as us because they were drawing cards. Campanella probably made two or three thousand."

Many of the players on the opposing team were Campy's teammates on the Dodgers during the regular season, and when they came to bat Campy, who was catching, would tip them off as to what pitch was coming. Leon pitched one game in Portsmouth and his old roomie from the Eagles, Leon Ruffin, was umpiring. After the game Ruffin sought out Day and Leon recounts the conversation. "After the game was over he said, 'Hey roomie! Hey man, you did damned good!' I said, 'You think so?' He said 'Yeah, Campanella was telling them every pitch that was coming.' I said 'You should have told me earlier, I would have crossed him up and them, too. I would have stuck that ball in one of them's ear.'"

After his barnstorming venture, Leon was back in Canada playing with the Edmonton Eskimos in the AAA Western International League for the 1953 season. He went back to Winnipeg the next year and finished his baseball career in 1955 with Brandon of the same Canadian league.

"I played 21 years, winter and summer," Leon reminisces. "I had a lot of scraps, you know, write-ups and such. I had a suitcase full and it all got burnt up in a fire in Newark." Like all pitchers, Leon took pride in his hitting, and one clipping that he remembers was one where he was leading the league in batting average. "I remember one time I was hitting about .450," he laughs. "That was the first part of the season and we had only played a few games. They put the averages in the paper, 'Leon Day was leading the league hitting .450.' I cut that out. I wanted to keep that clipping, because I knew I wasn't going to hit .450 long."

Although the fire destroyed the clippings, nothing can destroy the memories. Among his mental souvenirs is the remembrance of playing against Orlando Cepeda's father, Perucho Cepeda, in Puerto Rico. "Cepeda's father played with San Juan. I think he was a better ballplayer than his son. He was good enough to play in the States if he had wanted to." His memories are manifold and savored, but too many experiences have become ashes of the past.

Baseball was his life and he enjoyed every minute of it, but he knew when the time had come to call it quits. After deciding to retire from baseball for good, Leon went back to Newark and tended bar at a place called "Hodes". Happy in his work, he turned down offers for better jobs because he would rather just tend bar. Finally, around 1970, he succumbed to the lure of a different job, and moved to Baltimore where he worked as a security guard at a transfer company until retiring in 1979. Leon and his wife still reside in Baltimore and he maintains an active interest in America's game.

Leon Day, Monte Irvin and Ray Dandridge
at East Orange, New Jersey—1986.

The 1939 Newark Eagles with Leon Day (seated extreme left) and Monte Irvin (standing extreme left).

◊   ◊   ◊

Shortly after his retirement, the first reunion of former players from the Negro Leagues was held in Ashland, Kentucky and Leon was one of the first ones invited. He continued to attend each reunion until they were discontinued because of a lack of funds in 1983. The old war-horse enjoyed renewing old friendships and seeing faces that he had not seen in over thirty years. At those gatherings the calendar was rolled back while tales of yore were recalled and swapped about playing four games on holidays, changing clothes on the bus, hanging uniforms out the bus windows to air out while on the way to the next game, eating crackers and cheese on the run, and only sleeping one night a week in a bed. The camaraderie was strengthened as the years of hardships endured in a bygone era were relived.

Former players came from every part of the country to rekindle a love affair that they shared with the game of baseball. But baseball was a love that couldn't love back and the players got little in return except a heart full of memories.

Like all old-timers when they get together, as the years get more remote, the home runs get longer, the strikeouts become more numerous, and the memories grow sweeter. As sweet as the smell of the roses will be at Cooperstown for men like Leon Day when they are finally permitted to savor the fragrance of the long denied, but richly deserved, recognition of their forgotten greatness.

THE DEVIL

"The opposition would always say, 'Don't hit it to shortstop, because The Devil is playing out there.'"
Monte Irvin

WILLIE WELLS

Willie Wells was a battler on the baseball diamond, a scrappy firebrand who asked no quarter and gave no quarter, and whose personality and style of play earned him the nickname El Diablo in Mexico.

Today, retired in his hometown of Austin, Texas and living in the house in which he was reared, Willie suffers from a variety of illnesses, including one which has left him legally blind. He lives near members of his family including his son, Willie Jr., who also played baseball in the Negro Leagues.

I had spoken several times with Willie by phone but we had not met personally until I visited with him in Austin during the summer of 1986. Willie was lunching on fried chicken and listening to the New York Yankees playing on television when I arrived at his home on Newton Street.

The man who was known as The Devil was anything but deserving of that nickname on that hot July afternoon, as he cordially shared stories from bygone years. Willie preferred to talk more about his managerial skills than he did about his playing ability, and he feels that it is best to let others speak for him when discussions get around to his merits for the Hall of Fame.

"He belongs in the Hall of Fame," insists Judy Johnson, the great third base contemporary of Wells. "He could play. He played a shallow

shortstop like Boudreau. He'd get to the ball and get it away from him fast. And Wells could hit the ball. He was a really good hitter. He would hit with a bat that looked like it weighed a ton, and he could hit the ball against the fence. He could run and he'd move you out if you got in his way. He jumped on me and cut my leg open. Our team had to have special shin-guards made for the infielders. Wells was rough. That's how he got his nickname—The Devil."

Monte Irvin, who played with Willie, is another of the many who will speak for him. "I remember once when Willie Wells, who was our manager, captain and shortstop, said, 'Guys you know when we go up to East Orange, sometimes when we get in a tight situation they'll squeeze us.' He said, 'I'm going to use some psychology today.' He went up to the two umpires and he said, 'Fellows, are we going to have a good game today?' They said, 'Yes.' He said, 'Remember I don't want you to give us anything, but at the same time I don't want you to take anything away from us.' He did that to, in a key situation, get a called strike when it was right down the middle. And fortunately that did happen in the game, and it worked out just as he intended."

Wells' baseball ability clearly warrants him a place in the marbled halls of Cooperstown. "Wells had great hands and was a clutch hitter," says Monte. "He hurt his arm pitching and to compensate, he developed a knack for getting rid of the ball quickly. Before the injury he had a very strong arm. Afterward, since his arm wasn't as strong, he consequently played in real shallow. But he was great going back on pop flies. And what he lacked in arm strength, he made up for in wisdom. He was very smart about playing hitters. Because very rarely would anyone hit a ball that he couldn't get to. When he had to go backhand the ball and get the ball to first base, he'd get you out."

"He was a clutch player. He always came up with the big play or he would come up with the big hit. He was just as good fielder and a much better hitter than Pee Wee Reese. He was one of the best curveball hitters I ever saw. A very smart hitter. He was our lead-off hitter but he had good power and was a good hitter in the clutch. Pee Wee is in the Hall of Fame and I think that there's a chance that Wells will get into the Hall of Fame, too. I hope so because he deserves it. I just hope he hangs on a little longer. His name has been mentioned for several years."

Willie has become more reflective as the decades have mounted and now he thinks more about eternity than he does about baseball. Occasionally, he digressed when recounting the stories of his long and illustrious career, but the evening shadows lengthened much too rapidly as we passed the time reliving an era of baseball history.

As I was leaving Willie's home, he followed me to the door. "God bless you," he said, as I closed the screen behind me.

God bless you, too, Willie.

Excluded from the major leagues because of circumstance and tradition, black baseball players knew in their hearts that they were the equivalent of their white contemporaries and welcomed the opportunity to demonstrate this on the baseball diamonds of the Americas. "We enjoyed playing them. We used to play harder against them than we did against ourselves," explains pitching star Leon Day. "We weren't allowed to play with them, but by beating them we proved that we could have."

The proving grounds were the integrated leagues in Latin America and the post-season barnstorming tours against their major league counterparts who, playing before the era of million-dollar contracts, wanted some extra paydays to supplement their comparatively meager salaries. When the barnstorming major leaguers earned more per player than the teams playing in the World Series, Baseball Commissioner Judge Kenesaw Mountain Landis decreed that these exhibitions could not begin until after the end of the World Series. Perhaps because a majority of these encounters had been won by the black all-star teams, the traditionalist Landis had previously forbidden any major league team from playing intact against the select black aggregations.

When assembling a barnstorming all-star team from the Negro Leagues, the promoters chose the best players available. Thus, after the end of the 1945 season when Blanco Chataing decided to tour Venezuela with a black squad, he naturally wanted the services of the best shortstop around. That was a 40-year-old veteran who had been the best shortstop in black baseball for the better part of two decades. For over twenty years, summer and winter, he had starred in every league throughout the Western Hemisphere, including Mexico where he had earned the sobriquet "El Diablo"—The Devil.

The owner of his team, Effa Manley, called him "The finest shortstop, black or white," and the box scores recorded his name as Willie Wells, but those who witnessed his aggressive style of play agreed that the nickname conferred upon him south of the Rio Grande was more than appropriate.

Just how good was he? Well, if you were to take Ozzie Smith and unhinge the cannon hanging down from his right shoulder and replace it with the combination of Lou Boudreau's arm and knack for positioning batters, add .100 points to his batting average, and infuse him with a Ty Cobb level of intensity and competitiveness, then you would have Willie Wells.

Although Willie was well past his prime in 1945, when the other players learned that a rookie from the Kansas City Monarchs was being taken on the Venezuelan all-star tour instead of Wells, they were surprised. They knew that Willie, a proven veteran, was a superior

shortstop to the young Monarch who had earned his athletic fame as a
football player at the University of Southern California. The rookie's
name, of course, was Jackie Robinson.

The barnstorming team included Hall-of-Famer Buck Leonard who,
along with the other all-stars, had reservations about the selection, preferring Wells. "We had a whole lot of ballplayers better than Jackie Robinson. Everybody knew Wells was our best shortstop. Even if he was older,
he was our best shortstop." More questions were raised in the players'
minds when they saw Robinson conversing with Branch Rickey at the airport before leaving for Caracas. They knew that Rickey was talking about
organizing a new black team called the Brooklyn Brown Dodgers, and sur-
mised that this was the subject of the discussions.

Robinson, following Rickey's orders, told the players when they
asked that the Brown Dodgers *had* been the subject of their conversations.
Later, in Venezuela, when the story broke he told them the truth—that
Rickey was signing him to break the color barrier in the major leagues.

Most of the players were as surprised by Rickey's selection of Robinson for that role as they had been by his selection to the touring all-star
squad. Even greater than their surprise was their reservations about his
ability to play at that level of competition, and the corresponding ap-
prehension about possible adverse effects if he didn't succeed in the white
major leagues.

Robinson himself shared these reservations and had far greater self-
doubts than has generally been made known. His roommate in Venezuela
that winter, Gene Benson, spent many long hours at night encouraging
him and building his confidence in his ability to play in the major leagues.
Alluding to the variety of illegal pitches which was a part of the repertoire
of many Negro league pitchers, Benson emphasized to Jackie, "If you can
hit the pitchers in our league, you *know* you can hit in the majors."

Benson's moral support was typical of the players' response. Once
Rickey's announcement had been made public, they put aside their doubts
and united in providing support for the Monarch rookie. Although The
Devil was a better shortstop, Willie knew that his age was against him
and that he would have to be satisfied with the reflected glory. Like the
other great black veterans, Willie was glad that Jackie Robinson was getting the opportunity that he had been denied. Forty years later he still
remembers the emotions that were stirred when Robinson made the
breakthrough. "When they announced Jackie I was *proud*," Willie says,
still showing that pride. "The selection they made couldn't have been a
better selection." It is generally conceded that, instead of Jackie's baseball
ability, his education and experience playing with and against white athletes were the primary reasons for Rickey's choice. "He was a fine fellow," Willie agrees. "I was so glad they selected him because there was a

lot of blacks that were so ignorant. It hurts me to see another black out of order."

Just as desperately as the black players wanted Robinson to make good, they knew that he could not make it at shortstop, the position that he had played with the Monarchs. With Montreal in the spring of 1946 Jackie was moved to second base, which was better suited to his baseball skills. But, when the Dodgers made the transition, Jackie was concerned because he had never played the position before. When Wells talked to him during the spring, Jackie expressed his concern to Willie, telling him that he didn't even know how to make a pivot. Always willing to help a young ballplayer, the next day Willie began tutoring Robinson on the mechanics of playing the keystone position. The tutoring paid off as Jackie proved that he could handle the spot more than adequately, while also contributing a .349 batting average to the Montreal offense.

After a year's respite from his new spot in the infield during his rookie season at Brooklyn, Jackie moved back to the keystone position and two years later went on to have the best year of his career, winning the MVP Award while leading the Dodgers to the 1949 National League pennant.

The veteran Wells, too old for the major leagues himself, did get to see his protege make it to the top. Unfortunately, he also was present when the end came. Jackie Robinson's death, October 24, 1972 at the young age of 53, saddened the baseball world. Willie, living in New York at the time, grieved with the rest of the country, black and white. "I was at the funeral and after the service I went to the grounds," Willie recalls. "White kids were at Jackie Robinson's funeral. It was just so beautiful to see how things had changed."

The changes to which Willie refers are the country's racial perceptions. In the Jim Crow days when he was playing, black ballplayers were not only forbidden to play in the major leagues, but were also consigned to a life-style of second class status even while pursuing careers in their own separate leagues. The chance to escape these personal indignities and the promise of more money prompted Willie to pack up and go to Mexico to ply his trade. During his second tour of duty there, he expressed to *Pittsburgh Courier* reporter Wendell Smith the reasons for his decision to play in Mexico.

"I came back here to play ball for Vera Cruz because I have a better future in Mexico than in the States. Not only do I get more money playing here, but I live like a king. Some people look at my situation simply from the standpoint of money. But there's more to it than that."

"I am not faced with the racial problem in Mexico. When I travel with the Vera Cruz team we live in the best hotels, we eat in the best restaurants, and can go any place we care to. We don't enjoy such privileges in the United States. We stay in any kind of hotels, far from the best, and eat only where we know we will be accepted. Until recently Negro players in the United States had to go all over the country in buses, while in Mexico we've always traveled in trains."

"Players on teams in the Mexican league live just like big leaguers. We have everything first class, plus the fact that the people here are much

Willie "Devil" Wells
as the playing manager of the Newark Eagles.

more considerate than the American baseball fan. I mean that we are heroes here and not just ballplayers."

"One of the main reasons I came back to Mexico is because I've found freedom and democracy here, something I never found in the United States. I was branded a Negro in the States and had to act accordingly. Everything I did, including playing ball, was regulated by my color. They wouldn't even give me a chance in the big leagues because I was a Negro, yet they accepted every other nationality under the sun. Well, here in Mexico, I am a man. I can go as far in baseball as I am capable of going. I can live where I please and will encounter no restrictions of any kind because of my race. That also had a lot to do with my decision to return here."

Willie was the playing manager of the Newark Eagles when he initially succumbed to the lure of Mexico. He had first joined the Eagles in 1936 and was the hub of their famed million dollar infield comprised of Ray Dandridge at third base, Willie at shortstop, Dick Seay at second base, and Mule Suttles at first base. Although his arm was not as strong as some shortstop sharpies, he compensated for his only weakness with a quick release and scientific positioning. His superior knowledge of the batters enabled him to always be in position to make the play. Like his bowlegged sidekick on the left side of the Newark infield, Ray Dandridge, Willie would always manage to get the runner by a half-step.

Washington Senators' owner Clark Griffith, admired these two superb fielders and always wanted to watch them play whenever they played at Griffith Stadium. He once told black sportswriter Ric Roberts, "Let me know when those two bowlegged men are coming to Washington. Don't let me miss them." Dandridge, the other half of the Eagles' dynamic duo, has nothing but praise for his compadre. "He could field with anybody and his hitting was good, too," Ray says. "He was a hell of a ballplayer."

A proven winner who had played on championship teams in St. Louis in 1928, 1930, and 1931 and in Chicago in 1933, Willie proved to be the catalyst of the Eagles, excelling at bat, in the field, and on the bases, while also providing intelligent leadership. Shortly after his arrival in Newark, the team began winning and earned a lion's share of glory as they battled the Homestead Grays tooth-and-nail in one of black baseball's fiercest rivalries. "Every day I walked out there I wanted to win," Willie says. "I hated to lose and I worked hard. To be good at anything you do, you've got to work hard."

Hard work is what made Willie into one of the greatest shortstops of all time. He worked hard and played hard. His dedication and perseverance transformed him from a 17-year-old who couldn't hit a curveball into a lifetime .363 hitter. Aggressive and confident at the plate,

The 1939 East All-Star Team at Comiskey Park. Standing next to Willie Wells (second from left) is Buck Leonard (extreme left). Kneeling beside Leon Day (second from left) is spitball ace Bill Byrd (extreme left) whose beanball led to Wells pioneering the use of batting helmets. Hall of Fame slugger Josh Gibson is standing third from right.
(Photo courtesy of Buck Leonard.)

Willie didn't care who pitched or what they threw, he could hit them all. He thrived on pressure and was at his best in the clutch. When runners were on base, opposing managers would often instruct their pitchers to pitch around him.

Other times the managers would direct their hurlers to retaliate by throwing at Willie. "They threw at me because I was such a good hitter," he says. Grays' left-handed pitcher Edsall Walker, who often used Willie as a target, confirms this and recalls that when the Grays played the Eagles "everybody on the team threw at him except Raymond Brown. Brown wouldn't throw at him."

Some teams would threaten Willie to try to intimidate him. "They'd tell me all the time they were going to kill me," Willie recalls. One time the threats almost became a reality and led to Willie's pioneering the concept of wearing batting helmets.

In 1942 Willie was knocked unconscious by Bill Byrd, ace spitball pitcher for the Baltimore Elite Giants, and had to be carried from the stadium on a stretcher. Willie still carries the cruel memory of the beaning. "Byrd hit me in the head in Yankee Stadium," he recalls. "It hit me in the side of the head and they were worried about me."

Byrd remembers the beaning, too. "I hit Willie Wells," he declares. "I hit him in the head. The umpire said if the ball hadn't hit him, he would have called it a strike. He bent over the plate thinking I was going to pitch him outside. He didn't get back and a fastball hit him up side of the head pretty good."

That was on a Sunday and the two teams hooked up for a rematch in Baltimore the following Wednesday. "Byrd was pitching again," and although Willie was advised not to play, he insisted on being in the lineup. Prior to the game he went to a Jersey City construction site and got a worker's hard hat which he modified and used as a batting helmet.

However, that wasn't the first time that Willie had been forced to resort to a protective helmet. Buck Leonard recalls an earlier time in August of 1939 during a heated encounter between the two league rivals when Willie sought protection from potential beanballs. "At one game in Buffalo, Willie Wells wore a batting helmet for the first time. It was an old coal miner's hat that he had cut down, but it didn't have the light on it. Wells came into the ballpark with that helmet on and our big pitcher, Tom Parker, was pitching. We told Wells that Parker was going to knock that hat off of him." True to their boasts, Big Tom Parker's first pitch was right at his head. Undaunted, Willie picked himself up out of the dirt and slammed the next pitch for a triple.

"Parker was just carrying out what we had said when he threw the first pitch at his head," Buck adds. Edsall Walker also recalls an earlier time when Willie had donned a batting helmet. "The same year when I pitched in the all-star game, when I came back we're playing Newark in Buffalo and Wells rode with us in the bus from New York. So he jumped on me saying, 'We can't beat you and you go out there and let those guys in the East-West game beat you.'" Earlier in the year Walker, a hard-throwing left-hander with a southpaw's traditional control problems, had put Wells out of a doubleheader with a beanball in Wells' first plate appearance. And he warned Wells about castigating him about his all-star performance. "I said, 'Wells, you better watch yourself! I'm going to pitch against you some day.' He said, 'Oh, that's all right, I've got me a helmet.' So sure enough when we got up to Buffalo, Vic gave me the ball. So when Willie came up to the bat I said, 'Hey Wells, here I am!' He said, *'Throw* the ball!' The first pitch I hit him right between the shoulder blades. I told him, 'Hey, I'll bet you that helmet didn't do you any good, did it?'"

Despite their tactics Willie continued to wear the helmet when he felt it was necessary, and whenever they played the Grays the players continued to taunt him before the game, telling him that they were going to knock the hat off his head.

And the efforts at intimidation didn't stop there, it carried over to the base paths. From the day that he first broke into the league, players were constantly trying to spike the little shortstop. Willie remembers the threats and taunts. "They'd say, 'I'm going to get you out of there.'" But the little Devil fought back. He would "throw at their eyes" when they came into second base trying to take him out on double plays or he would apply a hard tag when there was no force play. "I'd take that ball and hit them right across their noses with it," the scrappy infielder says. "I went down to the river and got them little round bricks and put them in the fingers of the glove and hit them in the head with that glove."

He also got back at them when he was on the bases, going in with spikes high when the occasion called for protective retaliation. "You had to protect yourself," Willie asserts, still remembering the taunts. "They would be sitting in the hotel talking about it, saying 'Hey Wells, tomorrow we're going to get you. We're going to kill you.' But I was cool. I knew they were not my kind of person. Listen, they would call you dirty names and be filing their spikes."

"You've got to be tough," Willie continues. "But I knew who was good people and who was people who would do things to hurt you. I knew that. I would sit on the bench and watch them throwing at other players, or I'd see them trying to cut some of the other players. You've got to know how to protect yourself. Here's what I did. I was wearing those spiked shoes, kangaroo best, you know with the long cleats on

Buck Leonard, Dick Seay, Oscar Charleston, Vic Harris and Willie Wells at 1938 All-Star game. Harris, Wells and Leonard were the central figures in a spiking incident in a typical encounter between the Eagles and Grays.
(Photo courtesy of Buck Leonard.)

them. And what they were trying to do to me, I did to them! I had two sets of shoes, one for cutting them up and one to play." The ones he had for playing was the "best kangaroo feather weights." However, when playing the Homestead Grays he would have needed his other pair of shoes. Much like the Brooklyn Dodger-New York Giant rivalry in the white leagues, the Eagles and the Grays were always engaged in fierce competition. Knockdowns, spikings and brawls were commonplace.

In one Sunday game at Newark between the two teams with 25,000 rabid fans in attendance, Vic Harris, who was a "pretty tough fellow and a nasty slider," cut Willie's arm in a play at second base. "When a person jumps in the air at your body, you don't try to brace yourself against that slide or anything, you go with it," the spike-scarred veteran explains. "He cut my uniform off me and I had to go into the clubhouse and change. I was never a squawker," Willie says, "but I said to myself, 'The next time I come to bat I'm going to push the ball.' So when I came back out on the field, I pushed the ball between the pitcher and the first baseman. Vic was in the outfield, so I couldn't get at him. I'm going to do the same thing that Vic had done to me."

First baseman Buck Leonard covered the initial sack on the play, and Wells "jumped at him to cut him up." Willie explains, "Buck Leonard was my friend. But here's the kind of player I was. If you're trying to hurt me, I'm going to try to hurt some of you. Buck and I were good friends but I didn't care who it was who got in the way, who I had to make contact with. But I was trying to do the same thing that Vic had tried to do to me. And so after that happened Buck walked up to me and said, 'Hey Wells, I thought we were friends.' I said, 'That's right.' So Buck asked me, 'Why did it happen?' I said, 'You don't know why? Because you're playing with Vic and you're playing against me.'" That was Willie's credo. The aggressive little shortstop adds, "It's all right to be nice but if you play that way, I'll play that way too. But if you play right and clean, I did the same." Ray Dandridge confirms what Willie says, "If somebody played dirty against him, he played dirty with them. Back during that time it was dog-eat-dog."

"I jumped at Buck!" Willie reiterates. "They didn't like me too much and if you're good they try to get you out of the game." The man who played like a technicolor Ty Cobb is correct in this assessment. Rival teams' respect for Willie's ability and competitive spirit frequently resulted in him being targeted as the player to be put out of the game, one way or another. Not only because of his own aggressive style of play but also because they knew with him out of the lineup the Eagles would not be as formidable. Former Grays' great Buck Leonard, recounts his team's feelings about Wells. "We were trying to get him out of the ball game. Not that he had done anything to us. He was a mainstay in the ball game and we knew that if we could get him out, then it would reduce their strength. That's the reason why we were trying to get him out, not that we had anything personal against him. We knew that he was their best player and we wanted to get him out of the game."

"You had to protect yourself," the 5'7" 162-pound Wells agrees. "Just be a man. God made man, but he didn't say how big he was going to make him. I didn't talk, I just did. You don't talk about what you're going to do, you just do it. You knew you were wrong and that you did wrong. And if you do wrong, expect wrong, it's that simple."

Mule Suttles who was Willie's teammate at St. Louis, Chicago, and Newark could attest to that. Once in Cuba, when Mule was with Santa Clara and Willie played with Almendares, Willie pushed a bunt between first and second just as he had done against the Grays. On the play, the big hulking Suttles vacated the premises around the first base area. "Suttles *ran* from first base," Willie remembers. "He said, 'I know that dirty little S.O.B., he'd do that.'" The Mule was right. On the baseball field, Willie Wells asked no quarter and gave no quarter.

The bad blood between the two Negro League contenders erupted in early spring of 1942 when a beanball battle was followed by Wells' cutting Grays' second baseman Lick Carlisle, Josh Gibson jumping and injuring Ray Dandridge, and a free-for-all and near riot.

Edsall Walker maintains a different perspective about such clashes between the two teams. "It wasn't bad blood, it was just baseball." The left-hander relates another incident when the knockdown pitches resulted in a riot. "I know one game we played there and Newark's pitcher didn't throw at anybody. So his manager said, 'Throw at 'em! If you don't throw at him, you're going to get fined.' And we had a guy named Blue Perez up to bat. So Blue came over to the dugout and says, 'If this man throws at me, I'm going to throw the bat at him. And you hurry up and hustle me another one out there.' The first pitch didn't brush him back, he hit Blue. And Blue looks over to the dugout at Vic and says, 'Can I get him?' And Vic says, 'Go ahead.' And boy you talk about a race towards second base. Blue right behind the pitcher. Both dugouts emptied. One of the smallest players on the field jumped on Josh Gibson and Josh throwed him down and sat on him. And the next thing we know there are cops out there with horses." Buck Leonard explains, "They had to bring the horses out there because the fans got into it. The fans and everybody came out on the field and the policemen on horseback came out to break up the fight." After the law enforcement officers had things under control, the hometown fans threatened the Grays' players. Edsall continues the story, "And the crowd said, 'Wait until after the game, we'll get you.' After we got dressed we said, 'Don't put those bats up.' Everybody got a bat and we was ready, but when we got outside there wasn't a soul out there."

This story illustrates the emotional pitch which had built up between the partisans of the two teams during the season. With Wells leading the way the Eagles had beaten the Grays decisively that spring, and it appeared that Willie's team was going to dethrone the defending champion Grays. But two of his best players, Monte Irvin and Ray Dandridge, opted for the big pesos being handed out by Mexican millionaire Jorge Pasquel. As playing manager, Willie remained in Newark battling the Grays, and by mid-July he was leading the league in batting with a .423 average.

In recognition for his outstanding play, he was again voted to the East all-star squad for the East-West game. In the mid-season classic Wells was brilliant afield, making three outstanding stops. According to the reporters present, the last of these plays "brought the crowd to it's feet." In the sixth inning **Buck O'Neil** hit what appeared to be a perfect hit over second base but **Wells** "raced over behind the sack and scooped up the sizzling grounder and nipped him at first base by a step."

When the season ended, Cum Posey selected Willie to his annual All-America Dream Team. Posey, who as a player-manager-owner of the

Homestead Grays had been watching baseball since 1914, wrote that Wells "was a better all-around player than he has been in any year since we first saw him in 1927. That is saying a lot as he has been placed in the immortal class yearly."

Posey expresses the situation accurately, as Willie was already an established star dating back to the twenties and was virtually a perennial all-star after the inception of the East-West classic in 1933. Except for those years when he was playing outside the country, the veteran infielder was a fixture in the lineup and was selected a total of eight times. The Devil compiled an impressive set of all-star statistics, including a batting average of .281 and a slugging percentage of .438.

◊   ◊   ◊

Life for the man who became the greatest shortstop of his time began October 10, 1905 in a shack located in the southern part of Austin, Texas. Willie was the youngest of five children born to Lonnie and Cisco Wells. Because of the absences of his father, whose job as a pullman porter required frequent traveling, Willie developed a close relationship with his mother.

None of his three brothers played baseball but from as far back as Willie can remember, he had a ball in his hand and a love for sports. And baseball was his favorite. As a youngster, he would go to Austin's Dobbs Field to see the local squads play other ball clubs from the surrounding areas. One such team was the San Antonio Aces. Their star catcher was Biz Mackey, who would later become Willie's teammate with the Newark Eagles.

Mackey was from San Marcos, which is only about 35 miles south of Austin. Biz would let young Willie, a boy of about eleven, carry his catcher's mitt or equipment to get into the game free. Once inside the ballpark, Mackey would let the appreciative youngster sit on the bench with the players. Many years afterward as a veteran player himself, Willie provided a similar free pass for a youngster named Chico Renfroe, who was to later play with the Kansas City Monarchs.

Throughout his youth, Willie availed himself of every opportunity to play baseball and soon developed into one of the better players in his hometown. "I started to playing around here on the sandlots and everywhere around the country," he says. "When I got a little older they had a black league here in Texas and I went to Galveston." Willie continued to pursue his love of baseball but after leaving Anderson High School, his mother wanted him to go to college. Willie was prepared to follow his mother's wishes but fate intervened.

In 1925 when he was 19, Wells was a part of a local all-star group that played the St. Louis Stars and Chicago American Giants in spring exhibitions when the two professional teams trained in Texas. Both organizations liked what they saw in the fiery prospect and wanted to sign him for their ball clubs.

Rube Foster himself, the famous owner of the Chicago team, was vying for Willie's services. Also entered into the bidding were the St. Louis representatives, Dick Wallace and Dr. Keys, the owner of the team. "I was just so talented and I just loved to play and I had never been any place except right here in Austin," Willie explains. "But I couldn't go anywhere because my momma wanted me to go to college and finish school."

But Willie was determined to play professional baseball and continued in his efforts to persuade his mother to give him permission to go. When the first offer of $400 was made, it was more money than the young Texan had ever seen. Willie had watched his mother take in washing and ironing to make enough money to support her family and he thought he could help her through the "tough times" by accepting the offer and making some extra money. "I said to my mother, 'Momma, you've worked so hard and now I've got a chance to help you.' But my mother still held out."

Although his mother was adamant that her son attend college and many of the people around Austin told him that he wouldn't make the team, Willie was undaunted. Having worked previously "shucking corn and delivering newspapers" for pennies, the professional offers looked like "a lot of money" to the teenager. "Well, I didn't know anything about no money," Willie states matter-of-factly. "I was 19 years old, what the hell did I know about $400? I told Dr. Keys and all of them, 'It sounds all right to me but you're going to have to come out here and talk to my mother.'"

"So they came out here and talked to her," Willie recalls of the Stars' final appeal, "and they said, 'We know your son is young and everything and we'll take care of him. He'll be taken care of. He'll stay in our own home. You don't have to worry about him. But no money. We'll send you all the money and we'll just give him his expenses.'"

Finally his mother relented, but only after both managers promised her that Willie could attend college in the off-season. Choosing between the two teams was a tough decision for Willie, but his mother advised him to go to St. Louis because it was only an overnight train ride from Austin. So the obedient son chose St. Louis because it was closest to home. "And that's how I started out," Willie concludes.

When he first arrived in St. Louis he was told that they were going to send him back because he was so small, but Willie countered, "You're not going to send me nowhere." The hazing that the little rookie received was pretty rough. The players were larger and older and they would try to

The Devil played with the St. Louis Stars
for seven years (1925-1931) until the league broke up and the team disbanded.

intimidate the youngster. "They'd throw at you," Willie explains, "and they'd sit on the bench and file their spikes and say, 'This is for you, you son-of-a-bitch.'" But Willie refused to give up and, like Ty Cobb who suffered similar harassment, developed an aggressive style of play.

There was at least one veteran who did help the talented teenager. "A fellow playing shortstop there in St. Louis, Dick Wallace, taught me so much about fielding," remembers Willie of his early days as a professional baseball player. Willie's fielding was good that first season but he had difficulty hitting the curveball. Consequently he batted eighth in the lineup and the other players ragged him about his inability to hit the breaking pitch.

Despite his trouble with the curve that year, he and his mates finished a strong second to the Kansas City Monarchs during the first half of the split season and reversed that order to win the second half championship and force a play-off for the league title.

Willie still bitterly recounts the final game of the seven-game series. The game was played in Philadelphia on neutral grounds. "They wouldn't play us in St. Louis and we wouldn't play them in Kansas City," Willie explains of the neutral location. With the series tied at three games apiece, Bullet Rogan, the great pitcher-outfielder of the Monarchs came to bat with the winning run in scoring position. "He had gotten three base hits and Jim Taylor was the manager of our team and he said, 'He can't get four hits.' So they walked another batter to pitch to Rogan and he got the winning hit. Rogan went 4-for-5! I cried like a little baby all the way back to St. Louis."

The defeat was a disappointing one for the rookie, and after the series, he went back home to Austin for the off-season. To satisfy his mother, Willie registered at Sam Houston College. Although he didn't graduate from high school, they were going to let him take any classes he wanted. But the youngster was more determined than ever to make the grade in the Negro big leagues, and before he actually started attending classes at college, fate intervened again.

The Philadelphia Royals, a winter all-star team, sent for him to join them after an injury to Bill Riggins. Riggins, a shortstop from Detroit, had broken his leg and the team sent Willie a telegram offering him $400 to play with them in the California winter league. Again, his mother wanted him to stay and get his education but although she said "no" to his new opportunity, Willie slipped off without her knowing and went out to the Coast to play. "I didn't tell my mother," Willie remembers. "I got my clothes and almost slipped out of here. I never had seen California and I wanted to see California anyway. I told them to send the money to my mother and just give me expenses." So the youngster took the chance and never regretted it.

On the West Coast, the team stayed at the Dunbar Hotel on Central Avenue in Los Angeles. Willie stayed with the manager, who sent all his money back home to his mother like Willie had requested. "He handled me like his son," Willie recalls.

Aside from the money, Willie received something of even greater value. "I couldn't hit a curve," he remembers. Hurley McNair, an outfielder with the Kansas City Monarchs during the regular season, undertook the task of teaching Willie to hit a curveball. "He tied my ankle to home plate in practice so I wouldn't run away from a curve," Willie explains, "and fed me a steady diet of curveballs from the mound."

All the time and effort paid dividends for St. Louis in the spring. When the opposing players saw Willie coming to the plate they would yell "Here comes Ringers," and the pitchers, remembering his weakness from the previous year, began to throw him curves as they had before and he blistered them. "Every time they'd break a curveball, I'd hit it on a line somewhere, up against the fence or between the fielders." The manager took notice of the improvement and by opening day, Willie was slotted to bat third in the batting order. The sophomore shortstop finished the season with a .379 batting average, the second highest in the league.

As hard as Willie played on the field, off the field he realized the need to take care of his body and to lead a clean life. "I was in shape every day," Willie maintains. "I stayed in shape." Although not always successful, he tried to avoid hard drink, fast women and late hours as much as possible because "all those things are against you."

The clean living philosophy that he espouses today was shared by his roommate at St. Louis, Hall-of-famer Cool Papa Bell. The two of them would often sit in their room and play cards instead of going out on the town at night. They enjoyed a good relationship, which endured even after Bell married Willie's sweetheart. "I was crazy about her," Willie says of his first serious relationship, "but my mother told me not to marry her, so I forgot it that same day." Later when both Willie and Cool were picked to the same winter all-star team in California, he showed Cool her picture and some of her letters. Cool asked Willie "Are you going to marry her?" When Willie told him that he wasn't because of what his mother had said, Cool replied, "If you ain't going to marry her, I think I'd like her." That beginning eventually led to matrimony for the pair, and over a half-century later Cool Papa and Clarabelle are as much in love as ever. Meanwhile, Cool and Willie remained friends and teammates on the St. Louis Stars.

The two young superstars were joined on the team by a talented aggregation which included Mule Suttles, Ted Trent, George Giles, John Henry Russell, Frog Redus, underrated Branch Russell, and Dewey Creacy who Willie says "helped me a lot."

Willie characterizes the team in the beginning, as being "beautiful young players but we didn't know how to play. For two years in St. Louis, the Kansas City Monarchs would just kill us. But, after we got some experience and played together for awhile, they couldn't stop us."

Candy Jim Taylor, a veteran player and manager who was widely esteemed as a sound baseball man and was regarded as one of the best teachers of young players among Negro League managers, molded the character of the team while guiding them to their first pennant in 1928.

After the initial pennant the Stars lost the flag to the Monarchs in 1929 but battled back to cop the next two flags, which were the last in the history of the league founded by Rube Foster. In so doing, they supplanted the Chicago American Giants and Kansas City Monarchs as the dominant team in the league and were virtually unstoppable as they captured three pennants over a four year period.

Playing the most demanding position defensively and batting in the most responsible position in the lineup, Willie was the main man in the

Stars' success. His superb ability to make extraordinary plays on Texas leaguers allowed him to play a shallow shortstop. Veteran observers who saw both the legendary John Henry Lloyd and The Devil rate Willie as the equal of the Hall-of-Fame great. The comparison seems valid as both players starred in the tough Cuban winter league over a period of many years and the record shows lifetime batting averages of .321 and .320 for Lloyd and Wells, respectively.

◊   ◊   ◊

Besides excelling afield, Willie continued to demonstrate his prowess at the plate. He loved hitting in the Stars Park with the car barn in left field. He led the league in 1929 and 1930, with averages of .368 and .404. The former year he also led the league in hits and home runs, while the latter season he led in hits and doubles and finished second in home runs and stolen bases.

During the 1930 season, the Stars played Kansas City in the first night game ever played in St. Louis. Several major league players from the Cardinals and Cubs were present to watch the Stars defeat the Monarchs 4-0. The major leaguers, including Hack Wilson who was on his way to a record-setting 56 home runs and 190 RBIs, were surprised at how well the black players performed under the Monarchs' flood lights.

Following their initiation under the lights, the Stars traveled to Kansas City for a crucial weekend series against the defending champion Monarchs. Willie led the Stars to three victories in the four game series by hitting at a .375 clip and slugging out two home runs. Ignited by this success and with Willie leading the way in the field and at bat, the Stars continued their winning ways to nose out Kansas City by a half-game to win the first half championship, and later defeat Detroit in the play-off to secure the league's banner.

The talented young players were just maturing as a team and beginning to assert their superiority. Only the break-up of the league stopped them from establishing a dynasty. After annexing the league's final flag in 1931, both the league and the St. Louis Stars franchise folded and the players dispersed. The talented players from the pennant winning team were much in demand. "All those teams wanted me after St. Louis was breaking up," Willie confirms.

Initially Willie took his bat and glove and joined Satchel Paige, Cool Papa Bell, and Biz Mackey with Tom Wilson's Philadelphia Giants playing against Joe Pirrone's major league all-stars in the California winter league. But when winter turned to spring, Willie, signed with Dizzy Dismukes' Detroit Wolves. With Wells, Cool Papa Bell, and Mule Suttles from the Stars and future Homestead Gray pitching great Ray Brown

The 1931 St. Louis Stars. This aggregation won three pennants in four years. Seated extreme left is Willie "Devil" Wells. Seated fourth from left is Willie's roommate, Cool Papa Bell. Standing extreme right is Newt Allen who teamed with Wells to form a superlative keystone combination. Other key players were Ted Trent, Mule Suttles and George Giles (standing second, third and fourth from left, respectively).

forming the nucleus of the team, the Wolves forged into the lead ahead of the great Pittsburgh Crawfords in the newly formed East-West league with a record of 20-6.

However, the economics of the depression was still claiming victims and the Wolves and the Homestead Grays consolidated personnel for the remainder of the season, with the new Grays playing out the schedules of both teams. Under this new arrangement, with Wells leading the way, the Grays were awarded the first-half pennant in the East-West league.

Despite their success on the baseball diamond, Willie quickly grew disenchanted with the Grays' traveling conditions. "Traveling all the years I traveled, over those hills, you just got tired of it. At least I did," Willie says, remembering the constant travel with the Grays. "We played a game in Pittsburgh on Friday, and you know where we played the next day? Toronto, Canada. You know where we played the next day? Detroit, Michigan. Hell, I was in the clubhouse asleep and Posey said we had a game the next day in Detroit."

For three days Willie did not sleep in a bed, and never got to sleep before 3:00 A.M. "And he had booked another game about 30-40 miles out of Pittsburgh," Willie adds. When Cum Posey knocked on the door and said "Let's go, we got a game tonight," that was too much. "Not me!," responded Willie. Posey offered more money but money wasn't the problem. "I don't want no more of your money," Willie told him. "I just want my health and I want to live."

Willie left the Grays shortly afterwards and joined the Kansas City Monarchs where he teamed with Newt Allen to re-establish the middle infield combination from the 1931 St. Louis Stars, featuring the two greatest black players at their respective positions. In addition to this gold glove duo, the Monarchs also showcased the hit-and-run combination of Cool Papa Bell and George Giles from the St. Louis championship team of the preceding year.

This was not Willie's first experience with the Monarchs. "I played with Kansas City every year when I was at St. Louis. All the other teams in the league would want me after our season closed. They played so many exhibition games and things all over out in Minnesota and Iowa. All those places. So naturally I hadn't seen those cities, so when our season was over I would go to Kansas City to play exhibition games. I didn't do it later when I was with Chicago."

In late October, Willie made his first foray into Mexico when the Monarchs traveled to Mexico City to play their best teams, the Aztecs and the Gallos. Each of these Mexican squads had soundly defeated two invading white American teams. One of these was the Southern League champion Chattanooga Lookouts who had defeated Beaumont, the Texas

League pennant winner, in the Dixie Championships. The other team was a major league all-star squad. Neither American group could salvage even a single victory over the Mexican teams, so the Monarchs were not expected to dominate the local squads as they did. Wearing an American flag on their uniform sleeves, Willie and the Monarchs lost their first game but then, after getting acclimated to the altitude, ripped off five consecutive victories. Not only did their success make the American colony in Mexico extremely happy, but the local fans adopted the conquering Monarchs as their own. They were so popular that when they left the hotel, police and soldiers were necessary to keep the crowds moving.

◊   ◊   ◊

Meanwhile, back in the States an undertaker named Robert A. Cole had taken over the Chicago American Giants and was determined to rebuild the team into the baseball power that it had been under Rube Foster. Foster had become mentally incapacitated in the early spring of 1926, and passed away in December of 1930.

The legendary Foster had liked Willie since the first day that he saw him in Austin. From that time on, whenever Willie was in Chicago, he had a standing invitation to visit Rube at his office. On one occasion, Rube even bought Willie a Stetson. "Foster was a Texan, too, and he found out I was from Texas and bought me a Texan hat," Willie declares. "And I would go down to Indiana Street to his office and Rube would say, 'Hello, Little Ranger,' and we would talk." It was well known that Foster favored fellow Texans, and he obligingly passed on his baseball knowledge to the man he called Little Ranger. Willie appreciates all that he learned from Foster. "You know, I had so many breaks," he says, "and *good* breaks."

Foster wasn't the only one to make Willie feel at home in Chicago. The Spaulding factory let Wells pick his own wood and specifications for his bat. While most players used ash for their bats, Willie used only hickory. "The ball just came flying off that hickory bat," Willie says. "I didn't want no ash."

It was only natural then, that Willie would eventually sign with the American Giants. Joining him on the team were two other outstanding players, Mule Suttles and Ted Trent, from the defunct St. Louis Stars. Other key players on the squad were Willie Foster, Turkey Stearnes and Alex Radcliffe. Foster, half-brother of team founder Rube Foster, is generally conceded to be the best left-hander to ever pitch in the Negro Leagues. Stearnes was one of the most outstanding power hitters in the league while Radcliffe, the younger brother of the more colorful Double Duty Radcliffe, was the premier third baseman in the West for a dozen

Willie Wells as a member of the
1933 champion Chicago American Giants.

years. As a fielder he wasn't in a class with Ray Dandridge, Judy Johnson, or Oliver Marcelle but he was an adequate glovesman and a superb hitter.

With Willie providing the leadership, Chicago fought it's way to a championship in 1933, winning the first half title by defeating Satchel Paige and the Pittsburgh Crawfords in the deciding game by a score of 5-3. The American Giants continued their domination of the league in the second half, reeling off 28 straight victories throughout August. In early September, they again met the Crawfords in a crucial doubleheader. This time the games were played at Indianapolis, where Cole had moved the team's home games earlier in the season. Wells contributed a brace of hits in each contest as the two great teams split the twin-bill and, although Crawford owner Gus Greenlee contested the title, Chicago finished the season as champions of the Negro National League.

That was the year of the first Negro All-Star classic, the East-West game. At shortstop for the West squad was the catalyst from Chicago, Willie Wells, making the first of his three consecutive all-star appearances while playing in the Windy City. Although the game was played in an almost constant drizzle of rain, 20,000 people made their way to Comiskey Park to witness the inaugural of what was to become an annual event. Willie chalked up two hits, including a double to help the West squad to victory.

The scrappy shortstop repeated his superlative play in post-season contests as the American Giants continued to prove their ability on the baseball diamond. First, they defeated the Southern League Champion New Orleans Crescent Stars in a best-of-seven series. Leading three games to two, in the final fray Willie contributed his customary two hits, including one two-bagger, and was in the middle of two double plays as Chicago's ace left-hander Willie Foster won the clincher.

Next, they traveled to Redland Field in Cincinnati to defeat a major league all-star team, 3-0. Willie always performed well against major league competition, compiling a lifetime .410 batting average in those encounters. This game was no exception as Willie counted a home run in his pair of hits. Most of the opposing major leaguers played under assumed names but one who didn't was Willie's opposite number, the major league shortstop, Leo Durocher. Years later when there was much talk about blacks entering organized ball, Leo would say "Hell, I've seen a million good ones." Having played against Willie Wells there was no way that Durocher could have thought otherwise.

The following year the team made a valiant effort to repeat as league champions and were locked in a year-long duel with the Philadelphia Stars, who featured fireballing left-hander Slim Jones, the Lefty Grove of the Negro Leagues.

Early in the season with the two teams battling for league supremacy, Willie had five hits including two doubles and a triple to support Willie Foster's hurling as they downed Philadelphia 11-2. Sparked by Willie's leadership, Chicago copped the first half title. When the Negro National League released the first half stats, Willie was leading the league with a torrid average of .520 and had played errorless ball in the field. No wonder white sportswriters were referring to Willie as "the nearest thing to Honus Wagner that baseball has produced." Further praise came from Cum Posey who rated Willie as "the greatest money player in the game."

*The white sportswriters referred to Wells as "the nearest thing
to Honus Wagner that baseball has produced."*

After Philadelphia won the second half championship, Willie did everything possible to keep his team in the championship circle. In the fourth game of the play-offs, he doubled in the tying run and scored the winning run in a hard fought 2-1 duel. Despite Willie's heroics and Chicago's protest of two games for irregularities, they lost the play-off to the Stars.

Following the disappointment of the play-off loss, Willie and the team's two great sluggers, Turkey Stearnes and Mule Suttles, journeyed to California to join Tom Wilson's Nashville Elite Giants for the Coast Winter League. After another successful winter season, Willie returned to Chicago where he stayed until 1936, and was the acknowledged leader on and off the field. But after financial problems surfaced and the management offered Willie money to encourage the players to keep playing without a paycheck, he informed the players of the management's plan to withhold their money, quit the team, and advised the other players to act in their own best interests.

"I never went for anything crooked," Willie explains, recounting his exit from Chicago. "I didn't like the set up. They wanted to put my money in the bank for the whole season. But me, I didn't accept that. Willie Wells don't just think about himself. I think about other fellows on the club who are married and have kids and things. That's the way I think is right."

Instead of taking the owner's shady money to side against the players, Willie followed his own personal code of honor. "So in this office which is downtown in Chicago, with the owner, his secretary and everybody there, they said to me, 'They'll follow you, Wells. But You don't have to worry about your money.' That sounds all right, see. And of course they don't know what I'm going to say to the players. I told them right there in the office, I said, 'Well I'll tell you what you do. You call the players and have the fellows meet me down at the YMCA and I'll speak to them at 3:00 this afternoon.' Now he don't know what I'm going to say."

The owner thought that Willie would go along with his scheme and lead the players astray, but he didn't know that Willie Wells couldn't be bought off. "I'm not worried about me because I know I can play. That's the main thing when you know that you can do something, then if you think anything of yourself you've got to do what is right."

"Now when I got there the whole team was talking, saying 'So glad to have you here,' and things like that. But they hadn't heard what I had to say. The office didn't know, the secretaries didn't know, nobody knew."

"But what he said to me downtown that they were going to put my money in the bank for the whole season has got to be wrong. So what I

had to say was this. I said, 'I appreciate it that you fellows look to me as
your leader here in Chicago but I'm going to tell you this. You all had better find you another team to join and play with because I'm not going to
be here.'"

"Listen, you see, honesty is what really matters. I don't give a damn
how much money you've got. But if it's right, you're all right. But all that
other crap, you can have it, I don't want it."

So Willie left Chicago with clean hands. "That's when I went out
East to New York and contacted Mrs. Manley and her husband," he says
remembering those days. "I met Abe and Effa up on Sugar Hill, that's
where I went when I drove in there." The Manleys rewarded Willie's trip
by offering him a contract with the Newark Eagles.

◊   ◊   ◊

Willie had not been long in a Newark uniform before he began to show
the type of play that had exemplified his style since his rookie season in
the league. After his first year as an Eagle, Cum Posey selected him as

*Dandy (extreme left), Day (fourth from left) and The Devil (extreme right)
with the 1937 Newark Eagles.
(Photo courtesy of Jimmy Crutchfield.)*

the shortstop on his All-American Dream Team for 1936. This honor was
a prelude to the outstanding accomplishments of the 1937 team. In the
first game of a Sunday doubleheader in their home inaugural, Newark's
ace Leon Day pitched a four-hitter and received support from three-
quarters of the million dollar infield who showed their dexterity with a bat
to complement their gold glove performances afield. Willie, Ray
Dandridge, and Mule Suttles each had three hits apiece to pace the Eagles
attack before the home fans. Willie never slowed his pace and finished the
season with a .386 average.

The Eagles battled the Homestead Grays throughout the season.
However, after the last pitch had been thrown and the final out made, the
Eagles found themselves on the losing side of the struggle. Homestead
owner, Cum Posey, remembered their fierce contests on the baseball
diamond and picked Wells, Dandridge, Day and Terris McDuffie to play
with the Grays in a challenge series against a coalition of the Negro
American League's best teams. The Negro National leaguers upheld their
leagues honor by defeating a combination of Kansas City and Chicago
players, who represented the championship teams from their league's split
schedule.

Willie's hot bat continued on into the next season and at the end of
the first half he was pounding the horsehide for an average of .423. With
a sizzling bat and peerless glove work, he did all that could be expected
of a ballplayer. Ray Dandridge admires how well Wells did afield with
such a small glove. "Wells used to cut a hole in the middle of his glove,
and just have his bare hand there," he marvels. "He must have had tough
hands. I know a lot of times when those guys would fire that ball at him."
Willie maintains that the practice "helped me get a better feel for the ball
and made the ball stick in there better." The Eagle captain's performance
on the field pleased Abe Manley, who also recognized Willie's leadership
qualities, and eventually appointed him manager of the Eagles.

Throughout his tenure in this capacity, Wells was a players' manager.
"I would tell my team, especially the young players, in spring training in
Florida. 'All of the things that you fellows do in your private life, you're
going to respect it. And if you're going to make baseball your livelihood,
you must be able to sacrifice.'"

"There's this. I knew the weakness of each individual. Because men
are different. Some are strong. And I've noticed this, the weak try to follow the strong. You've got to evaluate your personnel first," Willie explains. "Some men are smarter, more intelligent than others. But a
ballplayer who is mechanical, you don't tamper with him." One of the
players that Willie didn't tamper with was Ray Dandridge. Ray was
mechanically flawless.

*Two great shortstops, Willie Wells (right) and Dick Lundy
both of whom should be in the Hall of Fame. This duo and
Hall-of-Famer John Henry Lloyd were the three greatest shortstops
in the history of black baseball.*

"I got along with him because I knew Ray Dandridge. You see anytime that you know your personnel, your temperaments, your attitudes, and how you get along with your teammates and things, you're ahead of the game. I don't care about how good you are. You've got to know personalities. I knew their personalities. I guess that's the reason that I had so much success in my managing."

"Here's what I didn't know about Ray. I didn't know he couldn't hear from his left side. I didn't know because I was to his left. He would be at third base and I'd be at shortstop. Before I learnt this, I wondered why he's ain't doing what I'm telling him to do."

"I know all the things about the opposite teams. In managing there's so much that you've got to know. You can't be guessing, you've got to know. I would watch all of their little moves and things. You've got to pick up all the little habits that they have. And when you know those things about the men you play with and against, you're on the ball."

Willie studied the opposition just like he studied his own team. He not only knew their strengths and weaknesses, but their tendencies and idiosyncrasies as well. He studied every baserunner, every catcher, every batter, every fielder, and every pitcher trying to find something that would give him an edge.

Then he would alert his team to that during clubhouse meetings and during the game he would control every facet of the game by giving signals from his shortstop position. Not only what pitches to throw but calling pick-offs and pitch-outs and positioning fielders. "I called all the signals," says Willie. "That's another thing that made me so successful."

Another factor contributing to Willie's success as a manager was one of his favorite players, Leon Day. Willie says of his ace right-hander "He was just a prince. He never complained about nothing. Everything was alright." And when Leon was on the mound things usually were alright. All any manager had to do with him was to write his name on the lineup card. Winners like Day made managing a much easier task. But while there were some like Dandridge and Day that presented no problems, there were many players whose temperament or lack of experience prohibited them from playing up to their potential.

His intelligence, insight into the game, and ability to instruct young players did not go unnoticed or unappreciated. Always a willing teacher, Willie passed on the benefits of his experience to younger players on their way up, including Monte Irvin, Larry Doby, Don Newcombe and Ernie Banks.

Both Irvin and Doby joined the team as infielders but he recognized that their future was as outfielders. When Monte Irvin first arrived as a hot-shot shortstop prospect, Willie told him, "I'm the shortstop here," and put Monte in the outfield. Later he advised Larry Doby in the same manner and when the major leagues signed them, they both were moved to the outfield and went on to outstanding careers in the big leagues.

He brought the overpowering, but temperamental, young Newcombe along slowly, laying the groundwork for Newk's development into the only player in the history of major league baseball to win the Rookie of the Year, the Cy Young, and the Most Valuable Player awards.

As a playing manager, Willie wanted to lead by example as well as by command, and he was at his best in clutch situations. A smart hitter with a good batting eye and great timing, who was known for hitting the ball back up the middle, he also hit with power when the team's best interests required an extra base hit.

To give himself an edge in the field the shrewd shortstop would watch his pitcher warm up prior to a game because he would play batters differently based on the type of deliveries of the pitcher. Then once the game was underway, Willie would flash the signal to the catcher from his shortstop position and position himself accordingly.

Willie was a disciple of the Rube Foster school of getting a run when it was truly needed. In the spring he would never let his pitchers throw to a hitter's weakness, but would wait until the regular season when it really mattered to take advantage of this bit of knowledge.

Wells was also a master at stealing the catcher's signs from the dugout and alerting his players to what was coming. He did this by observing each individual catcher to identify some tell-tale clue when they gave the sign. "I'm talking about knowing individuals. I'm talking about watching. I knew every action of the ball players. Josh Gibson had so much ability but when he would squat down to give the signals, his arms were so large that his arm would move. You watch his elbow and he would tip off all the signals. If I saw that, then it's a secret everybody in the league should know. It's so intelligent." An intense student of the game, Willie was continuously searching for something new to help his team win, and he endeavored to instill this same characteristic in his players.

As manager, he wanted absolute control of the team. In 1940 he had gone to Mexico to play with Jorge Pasquel because of money problems with the Manleys. After taking over the managerial reins, he again had some differences with the owners.

"I'd tell the office this," Willie declares. "'If you want me to manage the ball club I don't want players hanging around in your office because those fellows talk about a lot of things that they have no business talking about to you because you're paying them.' And a lot of them became stool pigeons. And I knew that."

Eventually Willie's disagreement with the ownership resulted in his leaving the team again. Like several managers of integrity, Wells had trouble with Mrs. Manley when he managed at Newark. But it was Abe Manley who was the actual cause of Willie's decision to leave the team in '45. Effa Manley often told managers who to pitch but in this instance it was Abe Manley who tried to dictate the pitching assignments to Willie.

"Now you see," Willie points out, "a lot of owners think they know as much about the game as you." In spring training in Florida Willie had spoken on Terris McDuffie's behalf in his efforts to get a raise. Although he resisted initially, Manley finally relented and gave McDuffie the money. "So here's what happened," Willie explains. "McDuffie was one of our pitchers and he had a lot of pride and a lot of ego and he was high tempered and very talkative and everything. You know some owners just don't like certain men. I say to myself, here I sleep with the fellows, I know their temperaments, and I know the feelings of each and every player. That's the reason you can have success as a manager. I know this is what made my career so wonderful, because the players would come to me. I don't care how good you are or what you do, you're not perfect. You make mistakes. But you're supposed to know about your personnel and I knew."

Early in the season, after granting the raise, Abe Manley wanted Willie to pitch Terris McDuffie although the skipper felt that he wasn't ready. In accord with Manley's wishes, Willie started McDuffie against Baltimore and he got shelled. So Willie took him out of the game and "Manley didn't like it. He wanted to humiliate him," Willie insists. "And he wanted him to start again the next day." But Willie refused to put the beleaguered hurler back on the mound when he wasn't ready. Instead he called the players off the field, told them what had happened, and quit as manager.

After this final disagreement with Manley, Willie turned over the team that he had assembled to Biz Mackey and they went on to become World Series Champions in 1946. The players didn't forget their former skipper and at their request, Willie sat on the bench during the World Series.

In spite of the circumstances under which Willie parted company with the Eagles, there was no lasting animosity. "Abe would send for me if they played major leaguers," Willie recalls, and remembers the last time that he saw Abe Manley. "I was in New York when he passed and at his funeral he was so small I couldn't believe it."

After his disagreement with the Manleys, Willie held the dual roles of player and manager with the New York Black Yankees, the Baltimore Elite Giants, the Indianapolis Clowns, and the Memphis Red Sox. "I didn't like the Black Yankees with Bill Holland and all those guys," Willie emphasizes. During the 1946 season he hit .297 while splitting the season between New York and Baltimore, and as late as 1948, at the age of 43, the wily veteran still pounded the horsehide for an average of .328 while with Memphis. When he finally hung up the spikes for good he had a lifetime average of .364 to show for his years in the Negro Leagues.

◊   ◊   ◊

Although barred from the major leagues because of his color, Willie frequently tested his mettle against big-league opposition in exhibition games. Throughout his career, the firebrand always welcomed the opportunity to prove himself against the best competition. In 1929 a trio of Stars from St. Louis, Willie, Cool Papa Bell, and Mule Suttles joined the Chicago American Giants to play against a major league all-star team. Among those playing for the white all-stars were Hall-of-Famers Charley Gehringer, Harry Heilmann, and Heinie Manush. During the post-season series, Willie made a distinct impression on the major leaguers by stealing home on two successive nights to win each of the games.

Two years later, the champion St. Louis Stars played a two-game series against a team of major league all-stars in St. Louis and won both of them. The major leaguers featured some high-powered talent in Bill Terry, Babe Herman, and the Waner brothers. Willie speaks highly of the white big leaguers. "They had a hell of a team! They had so much ball club that they had Max Carey playing third base. They had Paul Waner and Lloyd Waner and Babe Herman in the outfield and Max Carey had to play third base."

Willie also played against major leaguers in the Coast Winter League. In Sacramento, in one of his early appearances out there, he connected for a hit every time at bat. "The last time up I got a double and when I came back to the bench an old-timer said, 'Do you know who that is?'" The brash youngster didn't know one pitcher from another at that time. When he was informed that it was Chicago White Sox great Red Faber, Willie puffed up with pride. "My chest stuck out!," he smiles. From that time on, he felt like he could hit anybody.

In 1935, because of the after effects of the Batista-led revolution in Cuba two years earlier, Willie opted for the California winter league. There he played against a team consisting of Joe DiMaggio, Lefty Grove, and the Dean brothers. "Joe Pirrone had practically all major leaguers, you know," the shortstop sensation reminds us about the quality of the opposition. Although Willie hit .410 in exhibitions against major leaguers, he voiced his respect for the two hardest throwing major leaguers of the day. "Dizzy Dean and Lefty Grove, they were tough. I admired the way they could play." His admiration also encompassed the Detroit Tigers' great second baseman Charlie Gehringer. "Hot damn, he could play!" Willie says with respectful emphasis. "Charlie Gehringer was beautiful. Newt Allen was about the closest one to him from the Negro Leagues."

Looking back at that winter season more than fifty years ago, Willie also recalls the young DiMaggio, who was still a year away from wearing pinstripes. "We played against Joe DiMaggio in Pasadena," he says. "He hit it over those hedges. That's when everyone knew that Joe was ready for the majors." Willie knew all the white major leaguers who barnstormed against the black teams. "They knew me and I knew them," he says.

Still, Willie insists, the black squads won all 21 games against the major leaguers before Judge Landis broke it up, calling it "a disgrace." Landis may have thought it was disgraceful but the pitchers who had to face the best hitters in the Negro league lineup could have told him that to lose to players of their ability was nothing to be ashamed of. Still, some players were not happy losing to what was supposed to have been an inferior team. "Those whites didn't know we could play like we did," Willie explains. But, like Bobo Newsom who frequently barnstormed on the West Coast against the black players, they found out very quickly that the Negro league teams did play major league caliber ball.

Bobo was one of the players who didn't like losing to Black teams. "He was pitching in the winter league and we would beat him," Willie recalls, remembering Newsom as being "kind of prejudiced. He'd come right out and tell you, 'I'm not going back to the major leagues until I can beat you niggers.' He talked like that."

The black players also overheard Newsom repeating this vow to his white teammates. Willie recalls how his old roomie from the St. Louis Stars reacted to those comments. "Me and Cool Papa had lockers together. I was surprised by the way that he handled it. Cool Papa said, 'Well let's keep him out here about two years.'"

Beating the major leaguers was a way of proving to themselves that they could play in the major leagues if given the chance, but it wasn't the same as actually getting that opportunity. Several years later, although he was on the backside of his career, Willie almost made it to the big time. In 1944 when Bill Veeck was planning on buying the Philadelphia Phillies and stocking the war-time team with black players, Willie was one of the players slated to make the move into the major leagues. Among the others were Satchel Paige, Josh Gibson, Buck Leonard, and Ray Dandridge.

Even before Veeck's attempts to pull off the coup, Willie's exploits both against major leaguers and in the Negro Leagues had not gone unnoticed by knowledgeable baseball men. Two top Cuban major leaguers, St. Louis Cardinals' catcher Mike Gonzales and Cincinnati Reds' pitcher Adolph Luque, often saw him play on their days off. They were managers in their homeland during the winters and were always on the lookout for new talent.

"So Mike Gonzales was talking to Luque during the summer when he was with Cincinnati, and they were discussing the colored players because we were only allowed three imports from each team. They called us imports. They were screening the colored players. Mike would come down to our ballpark when they wouldn't be playing and Mike saw me and he told Luque, 'There's a kid down there in St. Louis, go down there and get him.' Luque was in charge of Almendares and Mike was with Havana. This is how my career in Cuba got started."

Luque, regarded as a tough hombre, was known to carry a gun to enforce discipline on his team and on more than one occasion he fired it to emphasize a point. Once Luque told Terris McDuffie to go into a game to pitch with only two days rest and McDuffie refused. Luque took him into his office, reached into a drawer and pulled out a pistol and asked McDuffie again if he was ready to pitch. This time McDuffie saw the wisdom of his manager's request and said, "Gimme the ball," and went out and pitched a two-hitter.

All ballplayers, black and white, knew that Luque was not a man to mess with. "Luque was a hot tempered Cuban," agrees Willie. On one occasion while playing with Luque's team, he saved another player from being shot by the volatile manager. "Double Duty Radcliffe was down there in Cuba with me," relates Willie. "I kept Luque from killing him. I only weighed about 165 pounds, but I had plenty of guts. See, I knew what type of person he was. He was Cuban but he was tempered and everything and would do things on the field, you know. I saw him pitching with the Cincinnati Reds and he tore a mound up. He was temperamental. You know what I mean? So I knew that. I knew his temperament."

"So here's what happened. Well, two people with tempers got into an argument. They were talking and arguing and Luque was high tempered and they came off the field and Luque had a pistol, you know. But me, I wasn't afraid, so I went over there and I got that straight."

Radcliffe, a colorful conniver, was given his nickname "Double Duty" by Damon Runyon after the writer witnessed a doubleheader in Yankee Stadium in which Radcliffe caught Satchel Paige in the first game and then pitched the victory in the second game. Runyon wrote that it was worth the price of two tickets to see Double Duty Radcliffe perform.

Double Duty remembers the incident with Luque and declares of Wells, "We played together eight straight winters in Cuba, and without a doubt, he was the greatest player I ever played with. We used to call him the vacuum cleaner."

Radcliffe and Luque may have differed on some things but they agreed on the merits of the little black shortstop who fielded his position like a vacuum cleaner. Willie tells of the additional responsibilities that the Cuban manager gave him on the field. "When I got there in Cuba, the first year now, and I can't speak no Spanish and had never been nowhere, and you know what I had to do? This is the job I had in Cuba. I had to play shortstop, and call all the pitches and everything. Luque told all the Spanish people, 'That damn Wells, whatever he signals, you do!'" And during the three years that he was there, Willie only made one call that upset Luque. "But, I was just smart," Willie smiles, "you know."

Luque had good reason to respect Willie's baseball expertise. In the 1937-38 winter season Willie coached an American all-star team against Luque's Cuban all-stars. The clash between the two baseball minds resulted in a thrilling 1-0 strategy session, with Luque's Island squad edging the American imports. A year later Willie was voted Almendares' most valuable player, and the following season turned in an even more extraordinary performance in his farewell season. While rapping the horsehide for a .328 batting average and being selected to a spot on the all-star team, he capped his career in the Cuban league by leading Almendares to the championship and earning the league MVP award.

◊   ◊   ◊

That was in 1940, the year when Willie chose to play in the Mexican summer league because of his differences with the Manleys. Except for the years that he played in the California winter league, Willie had played winters in Cuba up until that time. Versatile Cuban great Martin Dihigo, who could play all nine positions and is enshrined in the baseball halls of fame of three countries (Cuba, Mexico, and the United States) had seen Wells in action in Cuba and recruited Willie to play for him in Mexico.

"Listen," Willie says, "now I was in Vera Cruz because Martin Dihigo was the manager and he sent for me to come to Vera Cruz. We had a real good team down in Vera Cruz. This is when I first went to Mexico. And down in Vera Cruz it's so hot and all that water and stuff down there. And those mosquitoes. We had to sleep in nets. But, that's the only way to sleep down there in Vera Cruz. If you didn't sleep under those nets, you were in trouble, partner. I would wake up in the morning and the nets would be clogged with big mosquitoes, you know. After one year playing in Vera Cruz, our team moved to Mexico City. Mexico City was different." Despite the living conditions and mosquitoes, Willie managed to hit a cool .345 and the team ran off with the pennant.

Willie was as popular with the fans as he was disliked by some opposing players. "The fans liked him," agrees Ray Dandridge. In Mexico he was affectionately called El Diablo. Willie intimates that the beginning of the name was when a player said to him, "Wells, you look like you're mad about something." However, some players imply that his manner of play was the reason for the moniker. Dandridge agrees with this point of view. "You know, he's very devilish, on and off the field. He was really a devil when he was on the field. Most everybody who called him Diablo were the people who had seen him play. Off the field, he didn't do too much socializing. Nobody could get along with him except me. That was because we were both crazy! You know what I mean?" Whatever the facts surrounding the origin of the nickname, one thing is for certain, on the baseball diamond The Devil definitely lived up to his name.

In 1944, Willie made his second tour of Mexico when he replaced Rogers Hornsby as manager of Vera Cruz. As a youngster Willie had

*Monte Irvin and Willie Wells at the 50th anniversary
of the All-Star game in Chicago—1983.*
(Photo courtesy of Monte Irvin.)

watched Hornsby when he was in his prime with St. Louis, and he was a
little awed at being asked to replace the baseball immortal. "When they
sent for me in New York to replace Rogers Hornsby, I said, 'Oh my
God!'" Willie did not remain in awe for long as he took over the team
and produced a winning ball club. In all the years that he managed he
never fielded a losing team in any league. The Mexican fans appreciated
his style of baseball, both as a player and a manager. From his first year
in Pasquel's league through his last, El Diablo was beloved in Mexico.

The affection ran both ways and the Latin connection appealed to Willie who, in addition to the two summers that he played in Mexico, spent
five winters there. Most of his other winters in the Caribbean area were
spent in the Cuban league which was generally considered to be the
toughest loop outside the United States. During his only winter in Puerto
Rico, 1941-42, he recorded a healthy .378 average.

His former teammate at Newark and in Mexico, Ray Dandridge, also
played alongside Wells in Cuba. In the States the duo usually played on
the same side of the infield, but in Mexico and Cuba they played as a

keystone combination. Often, they would complete a double play from Wells to Dandridge to Wells to first base, or they would turn one out from Wells to Dandridge to first base.

In the winters of 1938 and 1939, he played on the same Cuban team as Hall-of-Famer Buck Leonard. The former year Willie bet Leonard, who was leading the league with a .400 average, that he could catch Buck and beat him for the batting title. Buck, known for only making bets that he was sure of, thought that with the margin of difference he could hold the lead easily and win both the bet and the batting championship. But when the last day of the season rolled around, he had to pay up because Willie had put on a surge and passed the slugging first sacker to cop the title.

All of Willie's experiences in Cuba were not as pleasant as this one, however. Even in a country where all ballplayers were accorded the same treatment on and off the field, racism would sometimes rear it's head. Some white Americans didn't adjust to the social differences on the Island as contrasted to the way they were in the States.

Willie recounts an incident involving Hall of Fame pitcher Early Wynn who earned his fame with the Cleveland Indians. "In Cuba, Early was pitching for Havana and I was playing for Almendares. He didn't like Blacks, you know" reminds Willie.

Willie liked to play the horses and the Island provided ample opportunity for this pastime. One day he and a white teammate, Bill Dunlap, stopped in at a cabaret to have a beer after a day at the Tropical Park racetrack. "Dunlap, who was from the Boston Braves, and I were good friends," Willie continues. "And we went to the racetracks and afterwards he said, 'Wells, stop in here and we'll have a beer.'"

The two ballplayers were sitting together quietly nursing their beers, when Early Wynn entered the Cabaret. Willie recalls, "Dunlap greeted him and said, 'Early come on and sit down.'" Wynn, who still adhered to the traditional social concepts of the time declined. "He said, 'I don't drink with niggers,' just like that," Willie continues. "It upset him, you know. He said, 'My father keeps his niggers on a plantation.' Dunlap got up and said, 'I don't have to sit here and take that,' and got up and hit Wynn. He tore that boy up bad. Wynn couldn't pitch no more the rest of the year. He really messed him up. That was in 1939 and I've done forgot all about it. I don't think about those things."

"I hadn't seen Early Wynn since 1939 until they had the all-star classic up there in Dallas. The Texas Rangers and Detroit Tigers were playing, so I went up there and Early Wynn was there. He was broadcasting for some ball club up there in Canada. So I hadn't seen him, and Early weighed about 200 and some odd pounds and I weighed 160 something.

So Early saw me and he ran to me and grabbed and hugged me. As big and strong as he was, I was *easy* to hug. He picked me up like I was a feather. He said, 'I haven't seen you since 1939.'"

Willie is pleased that times have changed so much since he was playing and that black players today can compete on equal terms in the major leagues and command salaries commensurate with their playing skills.

Like so many black superstars of his day, Willie was often told what he would be worth if he were white. Chili Gomez, a Mexican infielder who played briefly in the major leagues for the Philadelphia Phillies, approached Willie on the field one day and said, "Wells, if you were white, you'd be worth 7 million dollars. Boy, you've got everything."

Despite the Jim Crow policies that kept them from enjoying equal status, Willie would go out to see his white contemporaries play. "When we weren't playing I was sitting in the grandstands watching the Cards. In St. Louis, segregated and all, we went out there in Sportsmen's Park and watched the major leaguers play. I sat in those bleachers so many days and watched Rogers Hornsby, Pepper Martin and all of them. A few years later I watched Slats Marion." Referring to the grace that the Cardinals lanky shortstop displayed afield, Willie responds, "I admire good playing, and Marty Marion was so beautiful!"

Willie also speaks well of many other major league greats that he had never met until 1985 when he went to Cooperstown during the induction ceremonies. "I never had seen Pee Wee and never had met him. He was sitting right next to me. I admire him so much. Bob Feller and I were on the elevator and he knew me." Feller, who barnstormed against Satchel Paige's all-star squad from the Negro Leagues, has traveled extensively as a baseball ambassador and is one of the foremost white greats who readily gives the black ballplayers their proper recognition.

◊ ◊ ◊

Willie spent a quarter century trekking across the Western Hemisphere earning that recognition on the ball fields of the Americas. Most of his playing time outside of the United States was spent in the Southern Hemisphere, but south was not the only direction that Willie traveled to play baseball. He also played across the country's northern border in Winnipeg, Canada. "There were four ball clubs up there," Willie says, "and we had two black managers, Double Duty Radcliffe and me. I had a mixed ball club up there, and some of those players would go out and socialize and do things. And I didn't agree with the conduct and things some of them would do. Once some ballplayers got in a fight with some pullman porters over some women. The porters had them and the players wanted them. The league President called us in to talk to us about the incident. Double Duty said, 'I have a curfew on my men and I have rules for my men.' I said, 'Give me the names of the men involved and they'll be taken care of.' That's the way I did things. I don't believe in setting rules for grown men, and I wasn't going to put a curfew on the whole team for what a few players had done."

"They called me from Canada and asked me to get them a ball club. Minot, North Dakota had major league ballplayers and I knew it. I knew what Minot had and I went and got the best black ballplayers I could. I went all over to New Orleans and Memphis searching for the ballplayers that I liked their performance and their behavior. I told them, 'You've got to be a performer and you've got to be a respectable person.' And they would sit and listen to what I had to say and they'd say, 'I want to play for you.' And we won him a pennant."

When the Canadian baseball season ended each year, Willie would return to New York City. After his final season, when the veteran decided that he had reached the end of the line in baseball, Willie needed a job to support his family. "I was in New York and got me a job with a man who had a delicatessen on Nassau and Liberty," Willie explains. "When I applied for the job I never told them that I was a ballplayer but the papers headlined it."

"He said, 'I'll tell you what I'll do, we'll give you two weeks to learn this business.' I didn't know nothing. But in one week's time I did so well that I was with him 13 years until I came home. He saw that I was an honest man. You can't beat honesty."

"Mr. King, his wife and all of them wanted me to stay. But I said to myself, 'I'm going back to Texas.' So in 1973 I left New York and came back to Austin to help out my mother." Willie thinks that it was a good move to return to his roots in Texas. The crime and drugs in New York City were so bad that he was afraid to leave his apartment and go out on the streets. One particular incident that helped him make the decision stands out in Willie's mind. He was confronted face-to-face by a junkie who looked like he would have killed his own mother for the next fix. "That guy looked right at my *face* and everything," Willie says of the still vivid memory. "I made up my mind then to come on back to Texas."

"You see that is one reason that I came back to Texas. Because I had already met all the racketeers. All that money. That's what I'm talking about. Money didn't mean nothing to those people. All the rackets, all the cocaine, and all the pot, and all the pills. I've been with those people. Hear what I tell you. I've been in their homes and been with them and all that stuff. And they have the pots around the floor and it's so good to them, they have it in the pots. And the cocaine. I've been with the dealers and been with the people who have those habits. I don't see how in the

143

hell a person could use all that crap. They ain't got no brains. That's why I told you I was scared to death when I got back here. That's the truth."

"It's just a shame about those young black ballplayers, Len Bias and Don Rogers. It's pitiful. People are different. Their minds are different. Regardless of what you use or what you do, that's you, that's not Willie Wells. If there's ever been a person who was supposed to do those things, it was me. But I was strong. I don't have nothing to do with that. God was really good to me. He gave me so much talent, and He gave me knowledge, and everything else I needed. You've got to have good common sense, too."

◊   ◊   ◊

Since returning to his roots, Willie has lived in the same house that he lived in as a child. "This is the house I grew up in. Right here in this building. My brother and I slept together in the same bed." His son Willie Jr., who was also played in the Negro Leagues but without as much success as his famous father, also lives in Austin. But Willie lives alone now, and his health has not been very good lately. He has lost most of his eyesight because of diabetes and an assortment of other ills, and is considered legally blind. "People ask me, 'Are you bitter?'" The veteran of a quarter century in baseball declares, "Why should I be? I had a great career."

"We had so many great black ballplayers," Willie adds about the stars from the Negro Leagues. In recent years several shortstops have been inducted into the Hall of Fame, including Arky Vaughn, Pee Wee Reese, and Luis Aparicio. Still waiting in the wings is one who could field with any of them and out-hit most of them. His name, of course, is Willie Wells.

To get the recognition that he so richly deserves, and to be honored among the other great shortstops of all time, would revive the feeling that he had in his youth every spring when the new baseball season rolled around and he felt "like I was walking on cotton."

In recent years, more attention has been focused on the ballplayers from the Negro Leagues. On Tuesday August 2, 1983, the Honorable J.J. Pickle of Texas addressed Willie's greatness on the floor of the House of Representatives in Washington D.C. by reading the following statement into the *Congressional Record*:

> 'Mr. Speaker, as the greats of our National
> Pastime gathered last week at Cooperstown,
> New York to induct the most recent selec-
> tions into baseball's Hall of Fame, one very

> deserving name was missing from the list,
> Austinite Willie "Devil" Wells.
> Only one thing has kept Wells . . . from
> gaining the recognition he is due—he was
> born too soon.'

Representative Pickel then read from an article from the *Austin American,* dated July 6, 1983, detailing Willie's career and accomplishments. In the article, Willie responded to a question about his credentials for the Baseball Hall of Fame in typical fashion. "I can't talk about myself but other people seem to think so."

Cum Posey had expressed the thoughts of those other people in 1943 when he wrote in his column, "Wells is the best shortstop, day in and day out, we have ever seen. He can hit, run, argue, slide, catch flyballs in any territory, break up double steals, has the best one hand in baseball, and is the surest ground ball man of any decade. In addition to this Wells is a team man with a maniacal desire to win every game."

"You can know these things," Willie says of his reticence about boosting himself for the honor, "but you don't run off at the mouth." Since Willie keeps a modest profile, it is surprising how the chain of events leading to Representative Pickel's accolades on the House floor came about. "The way it started," Willie explains of the circumstances, "he was at his desk there in Washington and he was reading an article in the *Washington Post* about me. And he called the mayor here in Austin, and they gave me a beautiful reception. While we were sitting there talking, do you know what the mayor said to me? She said, 'Mr. Wells, you're so humble.' I said to myself, 'I've always been humble.'"

As he grows older, Willie's humility allows him to face life with a resigned acceptance of the order of things. "There's so many envious and jealous people," the octogenarian says, sadly shaking his head and staring into the dark of his blindness. "When you're in your mother's womb, God's got everything planned for you already."

Let's pray that what is planned for Willie Wells is to let him continue to walk God's good earth long enough to be able to smell the roses that he cannot see.

INDEX

149

150